Climate Finance Provided and Mobilised by Developed Countries in 2013-18

OECD》》 OECD

BETTER POLICIES FOR BETTER LIVES

This work is published under the responsibility of the Secretary-General of the OECD. The opinions expressed and arguments employed herein do not necessarily reflect the official views of OECD member countries.

This document, as well as any data and map included herein, are without prejudice to the status of or sovereignty over any territory, to the delimitation of international frontiers and boundaries and to the name of any territory, city or area.

Note by Turkey
The information in this document with reference to "Cyprus" relates to the southern part of the Island. There is no single authority representing both Turkish and Greek Cypriot people on the Island. Turkey recognises the Turkish Republic of Northern Cyprus (TRNC). Until a lasting and equitable solution is found within the context of the United Nations, Turkey shall preserve its position concerning the "Cyprus issue".

Note by all the European Union Member States of the OECD and the European Union
The Republic of Cyprus is recognised by all members of the United Nations with the exception of Turkey. The information in this document relates to the area under the effective control of the Government of the Republic of Cyprus.

Please cite this publication as:
OECD (2020), *Climate Finance Provided and Mobilised by Developed Countries in 2013-18*, OECD Publishing, Paris, *https://doi.org/10.1787/f0773d55-en*.

ISBN 978-92-64-39100-0 (print)
ISBN 978-92-64-68312-9 (pdf)

Context

This report was prepared to inform the international climate community about climate finance provided and mobilised by developed countries for climate action in developing countries in the context of the United Nations Framework Convention on Climate Change (UNFCCC). By adding figures for 2018 to the previously published 2013-17 time series (OECD, 2019[1]), the report provides insights on the evolution of the following four distinct components of climate finance provided and mobilised by developed countries over the period of 2013-18:

- Bilateral public climate finance;
- Multilateral climate finance attributed to developed countries;
- Climate-related officially supported export credits; and
- Private finance mobilised by bilateral and multilateral public climate finance, attributed to developed countries.

The analysis builds upon three main data sources, as detailed in Annex B: Biennial Reports submitted by Annex I Parties to the UNFCCC; OECD Development Assistance Committee (DAC) statistics on development finance; and OECD export credit statistics. To fill in a very limited number of remaining gaps, the OECD collected complementary ad hoc data from climate finance providers or developed estimates based on publicly available sources.

This publication is the third of its kind. It is based on the same accounting framework that underpinned the first two reports (OECD, 2019[1]), (OECD, 2015[2]) and is consistent with the outcome of the UNFCCC COP24 as regards the funding sources and financial instruments for the accounting of financial resources provided and mobilised through public interventions (UNFCCC, 2019[3]). Building on this past work, as well as on improved data quality and granularity, this report deepens the analysis by providing not only aggregate figures but also further, more granular analyses in terms of the recipients and characteristics of the associated finance provided and mobilised.

At the time of writing, the most recent information reported to the UNFCCC and the OECD DAC is for the year 2018. Table 1 summarises the time lags in the availability of the different datasets that underpin OECD figures of climate finance:

- Bilateral climate finance data for 2019 (as well as for 2020) are not due to be reported officially by Annex I Parties to the UNFCCC before January 2022, when the fifth Biennial Reports are due. The European Union (its member countries and the European Commission) has an annual internal reporting mechanism (Mechanism for Monitoring and Reporting (MMR)). Under the MMR, climate finance data for the previous calendar year are typically reported in October, e.g. data for 2019 were being reported at the time of finalising this report.
- Activity-level data for 2019 on multilateral public climate finance, as well as mobilised private finance, will not be reported to the OECD DAC in the required standardised format until later in 2020 as part of its annual statistical processes. After that, the OECD will undertake data quality assurance, adjustments (as required) as well as analysis to ensure data comparability. In the meantime, there are some published aggregate figures for climate finance provided and mobilised by multilateral development banks in 2019 (MDBs, 2020[4]). However, these figures are not compiled on the same basis as OECD analyses of climate finance provided and mobilised by developed countries, notably in terms of the point of measurement, geographical scope and

attribution. As a result, those aggregate figures cannot be directly compared to the figures presented in this report for "multilateral climate finance attributed to developed countries" and for "private finance mobilised".

Table 1. Time lags in the availability to the OECD of datasets needed to produce figures of climate finance provided and mobilised by developed countries

Component	Dataset	2018	2019	2020
Bilateral public	United Nations Framework Convention on Climate Change (UNFCCC)		Q1 2022	
Multilateral public	OECD Development Assistance Committee (DAC)	Q1 2020		Q1 2022
Export credits	OECD Export Credit Group (ECG)		Q1 2021	
Mobilised private	OECD Development Assistance Committee (DAC)			

Note: The timing indicated above relates to standard reporting practices. In practice, experience shows that some countries and institutions typically report earlier, while others experience delays.

The possible impacts of the COVID-19 pandemic include affecting the timelines of processes for some countries and institutions to collect and report 2020 activity-level data. As per the above such data are, under normal circumstances, not expected to be available to the OECD in a comprehensive manner until the first quarter of 2022, at earliest. Only then will it be possible to thoroughly assess the extent to which the crisis and its aftermath may also have impacted the ability of some developed countries to provide and mobilise climate finance, and of some developing countries to absorb and deploy such finance.

Acknowledgements

The report is an output of the OECD Environment Directorate, in close collaboration with the Development Co-operation Directorate:

- The analysis and drafting of the report were led by Tomáš Hos with significant contributions from Chiara Falduto, and under the supervision of Raphaël Jachnik as well as guidance from Jane Ellis and Simon Buckle.
- The report further benefited from inputs and comments from Julia Benn, Giorgio Gualberti, Nicolina Lamhauge, Cécile Sangaré, Haje Schütte and Jens Sedemund.

Michael Gonter (Trade and Agriculture Directorate) provided data on climate-related officially-supported export credits recorded under the Arrangement on Officially Supported Export Credits, as well as reviewed corresponding sections of the report.

Key highlights

This report presents annual volumes for 2013-18 of climate finance provided and mobilised by developed countries for developing countries in the context of UNFCCC processes. It adds figures for 2018 to those already published by the OECD for earlier years based on the same accounting framework. This framework is consistent with the outcome of the UNFCCC COP24 on funding sources and financial instruments for the accounting of finance provided and mobilised through public interventions.

The analysis is based on four distinct components: developed countries' bilateral public climate finance, multilateral public climate finance attributed to developed countries, climate-related officially-supported export credits extended by developed countries, and private climate finance mobilised by and attributed to developed countries public finance interventions. As such, the figures presented here do not capture all finance for climate action in developing countries. They notably exclude domestic and South-South public climate finance, multilateral climate finance attributable to developing countries, as well as private finance invested in the absence of developed countries' public finance interventions.

The year-on-year time series is consistent from 2013 to 2018 for bilateral and multilateral public climate finance as well as for export credits. Therefore, for these three components, the report presents analyses over 2013-18. In contrast, figures for mobilised private climate finance from 2016 onwards are not directly comparable with those for 2013-14 due to the implementation of enhanced measurement methods and a resulting gap in the time series in 2015. As a result, analyses of total climate finance provided and mobilised by developed countries, and of the mobilised private climate finance component focus on 2016-18.

Aggregate trends

- Total climate finance provided and mobilised by developed countries for developing countries reached USD 78.9 billion in 2018, up by 11% from USD 71.2 billion in 2017. This represents a slower growth rate than the 22% rise from 2016 (USD 58.6 billion) to 2017.

- Within this total, public climate finance provided by developed countries increased from USD 37.9 billion in 2013 to USD 62.2 billion in 2018, excluding climate-related officially-supported export credits. This rises to USD 64.3 billion in 2018 when including export credits.
  - Bilateral public climate finance reached USD 32.7 billion in 2018, accounting for the largest share of the 2018 total. This represents a rise of USD 5.7 billion (+21%) from 2017. Since 2013, this component has increased on average by USD 2 billion per year.
  - Multilateral public climate finance attributed to developed countries totalled USD 29.6 billion in 2018. This figure is USD 2.1 billion more (+8%) than in 2017. Since 2013, this component has increased on average by USD 2.8 billion per year.
  - Officially-supported export credits remained a small component, amounting to USD 2.1 billion in 2018. The annual average level over 2013-18 was USD 1.9 billion.

- Private climate finance mobilised attributed to developed countries stabilised at USD 14.6 billion in 2018. This is USD 0.1 billion more than in 2017, when it reached USD 14.5 billion after growing from USD 10.1 billion in 2016. The annual average increase over 2016-18 was USD 2.2 billion.

Table 2. Climate finance provided and mobilised by developed countries (2013-18, USD billion)

	2013	2014	2015	2016	2017	2018
Bilateral public climate finance (1)	22.5	23.1	25.9	28.0	27.0	32.7
Multilateral public climate finance attributable to developed countries (2)	15.5	20.4	16.2	18.9	27.5	29.6
Subtotal (1+2)	**37.9**	**43.5**	**42.1**	**46.9**	**54.5**	**62.2**
Climate-related officially-supported export credits (3)	1.6	1.6	2.5	1.5	2.1	2.1
Subtotal (1+2+3)	**39.5**	**45.1**	**44.6**	**48.5**	**56.7**	**64.3**
Private climate finance mobilised (4)	12.8	16.7	N/A	10.1	14.5	14.6
By bilateral public climate finance	6.5	8.1	N/A	5.0	3.7	3.8
By multilateral public climate finance attributable to developed countries	6.2	8.6	N/A	5.1	10.8	10.8
Grand Total (1+2+3+4)	**52.2**	**61.8**	**N/A**	**58.6**	**71.2**	**78.9**

Note: The sum of components may not add up to totals due to rounding. The gap in time series in 2015 for mobilised private finance results from the implementation of enhanced measurement methods. As a result, grand totals in 2016-18 and in 2013-14 are not directly comparable.
Source: based on Biennial Reports to the UNFCCC, OECD Development Assistance Committee statistics, OECD Export Credit Group statistics, as well as complementary reporting to the OECD.

Breakdowns by climate focus, instrument, and sector

- Over 2016-18, total mitigation and adaptation finance provided and mobilised by developed countries each followed an increasing trend. Finance for adaptation grew by 29% per year on average to reach USD 16.8 billion in 2018, while finance for mitigation grew by 15% per year on average and more in absolute terms, reaching USD 55 billion in 2018. Mitigation continues to represent over two-thirds (70%) of the 2018 total, adaptation 21%, and cross-cutting the remainder.

- In terms of the financial instruments that underpin public climate finance provided by developed countries (both bilaterally and via multilateral institutions), loans more than doubled from USD 19.8 billion in 2013 to USD 46.3 billion in 2018. Grants fluctuated around USD 10 billion per year in 2013-15 and around USD 12 billion in 2016-18. As a result, between 2013 and 2018, the share of loans in total public finance provided grew from 52% to 74%, while the share of grants decreased from 27% to 20%. Equity investments increased from USD 0.7 billion in 2013 to USD 1.1 billion in 2018, accounting for 2% of public climate finance.

- The largest share of total climate finance provided and mobilised over 2016-18 was for energy (34%), followed by transport and storage (14%), agriculture, forestry and fishing (9%) and water and sanitation (7%). Mitigation finance dominated the energy and transport sectors. The share of adaptation finance was most prominent in the water and sanitation, and agriculture sectors.

Geographic breakdown

- Over 2016-18, Asia benefitted from the largest share (43%) of total climate finance provided and mobilised by developed countries, followed by Africa (25%), the Americas (17%), non-EU/EEA Europe (4%) and Oceania (1%). The remainder (10%) was, at the point of reporting, unspecified or targeted multiple regions. At the sub-regional level, highly populated areas, such as South and East Asia or South America, were allocated the largest shares (18%, 13% and 12%, respectively).

- In 2016-18, 79% of total climate finance provided and mobilised by developed countries reported as allocated to individual countries, while 21% was reported at regional level or for multiple countries. Financing for Least Developed Countries (LDCs) and Small Island Developing States (SIDS) represented 14% and 2% of the total, respectively. In terms of distribution by income group, 69% was for middle-income countries (MICs), 8% for low-income countries (LICs) and 2% for a limited number of high-income countries (HICs) included in the geographical scope of this analysis.

- In terms of climate finance per capita, SIDS and other countries with a relatively small population were the highest recipients in 2016-18. Out of the top 25 per capita recipients, 21 were SIDS. The other four have a population of less than 10 million. Regions and sub-regions with a relatively small population, including Oceania, non-EU/EEA Europe, and Central Asia benefitted from over USD 20 per capita, as did Northern Africa and South America. Highly populated sub-regions, such as East and South Asia, West and Central Africa, benefitted from less than USD 10 per capita.

- The focus of climate finance in LICs differs substantially than for developing countries on average, with adaptation, grant financing, the water and sanitation and agriculture sectors, all representing higher shares of climate finance provided and mobilised in 2016-18. In contrast, mitigation activities, the energy and transport sectors, loans and private finance mobilised, all represented higher shares for MICs than for all developing countries on average.

Characteristics of private climate finance mobilised

- Private climate finance mobilised by developed countries during 2016-18 focused almost only on climate mitigation (93%), targeted mainly the energy sector (60% of the total) and mainly benefitted MICs (69%). In contrast, adaptation, the agriculture sector and LICs accounted for much lower shares. Asia (44%), the Americas (25%) and Africa (17%) were the main beneficiary regions.

- During 2016-18, developed countries mobilised private climate finance mainly through direct investment in companies or project finance special purpose vehicles (SPVs), guarantees and syndicated loans:
  - Private climate finance mobilised via guarantees and syndicated loans grew in absolute and relative terms over the three years to reach 31% (USD 4.5 billion) and 19% (USD 2.8 billion) respectively of the USD 14.6 billion total in 2018.
  - Mobilisation through direct investment in companies or SPVs declined in absolute and relative terms over the three years but remained the largest mobilisation mechanism in 2018 (USD 4.8 billion; 33% of the total).
  - Credit lines (USD 0.9 billion in 2018), investments in funds (USD 0.8 billion), and simple co-financing arrangements (USD 0.8 billion) accounted, together, for just under 20% of mobilised private climate finance in each year.

Data and methodological considerations

- The availability and quality of data have improved over time. However, a number of challenges remain to further improve data quality and accessibility. For instance, country reporting of bilateral climate finance data to the UNFCCC in an improved machine-readable and harmonised format would limit errors and increase the efficiency of subsequent analytical processes.

- Comparability of data helps avoid double counting. Some standardisation can take place within each country's data collection processes and across institutions (e.g. Multilateral Development Banks). International statistical standards, such as those of the OECD Development Assistance Committee (DAC), however, play a crucial role in improving data comparability and consistency.

- Reporting climate finance at the level of individual activities maximises the quality and robustness of analyses, and helps build trust between recipient and provider countries. With this in mind:
  - Public climate finance providers, both bilateral and multilateral, could provide further transparency on the share of individual projects that they assess and report as being climate-relevant, so as to address potential concerns of over-reporting and facilitate third party reviews.
  - Data providers and recipients could further collaborate to address confidentiality issues, particularly those relating to mobilised private finance, in a way that enables the international community to access information at the level of detail necessary to inform policy processes.

Infographic 1. Climate finance provided and mobilised by developed countries (2016-18, %)

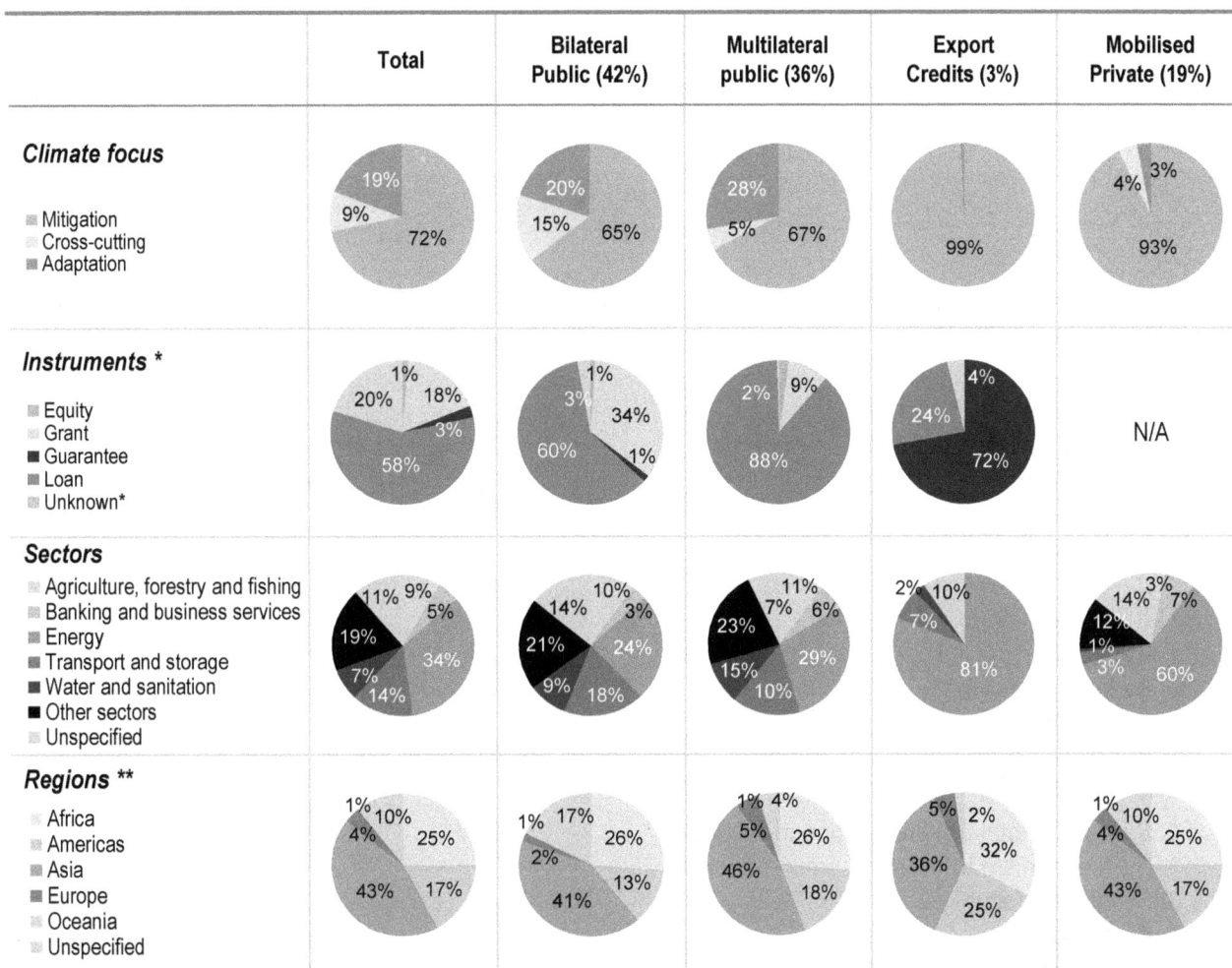

	Total	Bilateral Public (42%)	Multilateral public (36%)	Export Credits (3%)	Mobilised Private (19%)
Climate focus ▪ Mitigation ▪ Cross-cutting ▪ Adaptation	19% / 9% / 72%	20% / 15% / 65%	28% / 5% / 67%	99%	4% / 3% / 93%
Instruments * ▪ Equity ▪ Grant ▪ Guarantee ▪ Loan ▪ Unknown*	1% / 20% / 18% / 3% / 58%	1% / 3% / 34% / 1% / 60%	9% / 2% / 88% / 2%	4% / 24% / 72%	N/A
Sectors ▪ Agriculture, forestry and fishing ▪ Banking and business services ▪ Energy ▪ Transport and storage ▪ Water and sanitation ▪ Other sectors ▪ Unspecified	11% / 9% / 5% / 34% / 14% / 7% / 19%	10% / 3% / 24% / 18% / 9% / 21% / 14%	11% / 7% / 6% / 29% / 10% / 15% / 23%	2% / 10% / 81% / 7%	3% / 7% / 60% / 3% / 1% / 12% / 14%
Regions ** ▪ Africa ▪ Americas ▪ Asia ▪ Europe ▪ Oceania ▪ Unspecified	1% / 10% / 25% / 17% / 43% / 4%	1% / 17% / 26% / 13% / 41% / 2%	1% / 4% / 26% / 18% / 46% / 5%	5% / 2% / 32% / 25% / 36%	1% / 10% / 25% / 17% / 43% / 4%

* For financial instruments, "unknown" includes unspecified public finance as well as all mobilised private climate finance.

** Each of the regions only includes developing countries as defined in Annex 3 of this report.

Source: Based on Biennial Reports to the UNFCCC, OECD Development Assistance Committee statistics, OECD Export Credit Group statistics, as well as complementary reporting to the OECD.

Table of contents

Tables

Figures

Boxes

1 Aggregate trends

This chapter highlights the evolution of annual levels of climate finance provided and mobilised by developed countries for developing countries in 2013-18 in the context of the United National Framework Convention on Climate Change (UNFCCC). This chapter first presents an overview of main trends, followed by more detailed analyses presented by climate focus, financial instrument, and sector.

The accounting framework for this analysis is consistent with that used in the previous two OECD reports on climate finance provided and mobilised by developed countries for developing countries (OECD, 2019[1]; OECD, 2015[2]), and on related climate finance projections (OECD, 2016[3]). The framework is also aligned with the outcome of the UNFCCC COP24 on funding sources and financial instruments for the accounting of financial resources provided and mobilised through public interventions (UNFCCC, 2019[4]). The analysis is based on four distinct components:

- Bilateral public climate finance;
- Multilateral public climate finance attributed to developed countries;
- Climate-related officially-supported export credits; and
- Private climate finance mobilised by bilateral and multilateral public finance, attributed to developed countries.

Figures for the first three components are calculated using consistent methodologies and datasets over 2013-18, complemented with estimates where needed (e.g. one-off partial data gaps in specific years). For these three components, the report, therefore, presents analyses over 2013-18.

In contrast, methods and data that underpin the mobilised private finance component significantly evolved over time, reaching greater maturity in more recent years. The private climate finance figures for 2013-14, which were estimated based on best available (sometimes semi-aggregate) co-financing data from providers at the time (OECD, 2015[2]), are not directly comparable with data for 2016 onwards. As explained in (OECD, 2019[1]) and summarised in Annex B of the present report, the latter are based on improved methods and standardised activity-level data collected on that basis by the OECD DAC (OECD, 2020[5]). The progressive implementation of these improved methods, including in terms of climate marking of mobilised private finance data, results in a data gap in the time series in 2015. Hence, analyses of total climate finance provided and mobilised by developed countries and of the mobilised private climate finance component focus on the period 2016-18.

The climate finance figures presented in this report do not capture all finance for climate action in developing countries. Due to the geographical scope, the figures include neither developing countries domestic public climate finance, nor bilateral public climate finance between developing countries in the context of the so-called "South-South" cooperation, nor multilateral and mobilised private climate finance attributable to developing countries themselves. Further, the figures presented include neither private finance catalysed by public policy interventions, for which there remains a lack of measurement methodology, nor private finance invested in the absence of public interventions altogether.

1.1. Overview across the four components

Since 2013, total climate finance provided and mobilised by developed countries has increased, reaching USD 78.9 billion in 2018. Over the period of 2016-18, for which the total volumes are comparable, climate finance grew by 22% between 2016 and 2017 (from USD 58.6 billion to USD 71.2 billion) and by 11% between 2017 and 2018 (Figure 1.1).

Public climate finance represents the largest share of total climate finance provided and mobilised, reaching USD 62.2 (79% of the total) in 2018, and is the main driver of the overall rising trend since 2013. This observation applies to both the bilateral and the multilateral climate finance components, which together constitute more than three-quarters of the annual totals in 2016-18. In particular:

- Bilateral climate finance has followed an upward trend over the six-year period despite a slight drop in 2017. In 2018, bilateral public climate finance reached USD 32.7 billion, the highest volume for this component during the period covered, representing a 45% increase compared to 2013 (USD 22.5 billion). Since 2013, bilateral public climate finance has increased on average by USD 2 billion per year.
- Multilateral climate finance attributed to developed countries has been increasing too, despite a drop in 2015, with the 2018 figure (USD 29.6 billion) reaching almost double its 2013 value (USD 15.5 billion). Since 2013, multilateral public climate finance increased on average by USD 2.8 billion per year.

Figure 1.1. Climate finance provided and mobilised (2013-18, USD billion)

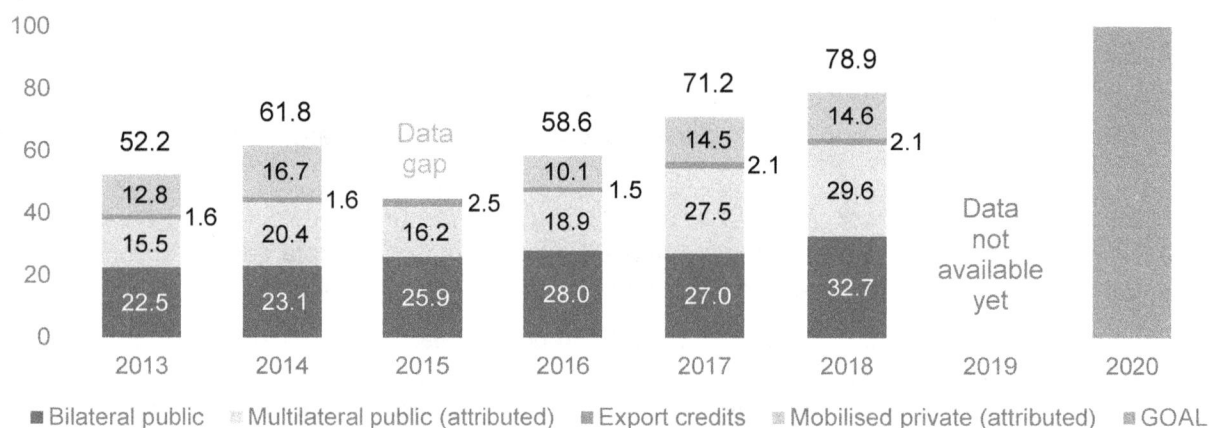

Note: "Multilateral public" does not represent total outflows from multilateral institutions to developing countries but only the share calculated by the OECD as attributable to developed countries. The data gap in 2015 for mobilised private finance results from the implementation of enhanced measurement methods (see (OECD DAC, 2020[6]). As a result, grand totals in 2016-17 and in 2013-14 are not directly comparable.
Source: based on Biennial Reports to the UNFCCC, OECD Development Assistance Committee statistics, OECD Export Credit Group statistics, as well as complementary reporting to the OECD.

Volumes of officially-supported export credits and mobilised private climate finance fluctuated throughout the period, including due to variations in annual commitments. Given the increase in public climate finance, both components represent a smaller share of total climate finance in 2018 compared to 2017 and 2016.

Officially-supported export credits (guarantees and loans, see Annex B) for climate-related activities fluctuated around an average of USD 2 billion per year since 2013. They represent a small and decreasing share of the total climate finance provided and mobilised. This trend may be in part due to the difficulties in comprehensively tracking climate-related export credits, in particular in capturing relevant activities beyond the renewable energy sector (Annex B).

Private climate finance mobilised by developed countries grew by USD 4.4 billion (43%) between 2016 and 2017; i.e. from USD 10.1 billion to USD 14.5 billion. Between 2017 and 2018 it increased by USD 0.1 billion. Chapter 3 provides further analyses of mobilised private climate finance, including in contrast to private finance mobilised for non-climate projects.

1.2. Thematic split

Over the period of 2016-18, for which the grand totals are comparable, climate finance targeting mitigation and adaptation objectives was on the rise on a year-by-year basis (Figure 1.2). Adaptation finance grew by an annual average of 29%, from USD 10.1 billion in 2016 to USD 16.8 billion in 2018. However, tracking finance for climate change adaptation remains challenging, as highlighted in Box 1.1. Mitigation finance increased mainly from 2016 to 2017 when it grew from USD 42.2 billion to USD 52.3 billion (+24%), and subsequently more modestly to reach USD 55 billion in 2018 (i.e. an annual average growth of 15%). Finance for cross-cutting objectives (which is mostly reported by bilateral providers, much less so by multilateral institutions) first decreased from USD 6.2 billion in 2016 to USD 5.5 billion in 2017 but rose subsequently in 2018, when it reached USD 7.1 billion (an increase of 15% from 2016).

Figure 1.2. Thematic split of climate finance provided and mobilised (2013-18, USD billion)

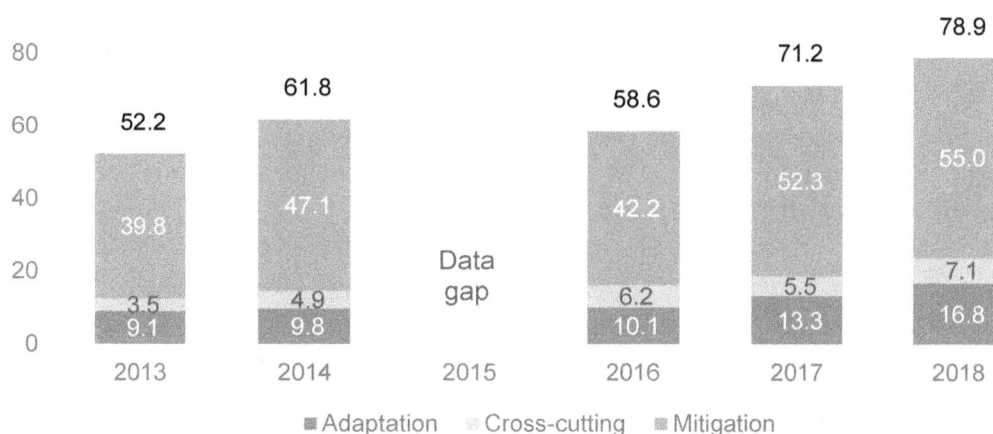

Source: based on Biennial Reports to the UNFCCC, OECD Development Assistance Committee statistics, as well as complementary reporting to the OECD.

In relative terms, mitigation continues to represent over two-thirds of total climate finance provided and mobilised. Adaptation finance, however, grew slightly in relative terms, from 17% in 2016 to 21% in 2018 Figure 1.2. Finance for cross-cutting activities fluctuated slightly between a minimum of 7% of the total and a maximum of 11% of the total over the 2013-18 period.

Box 1.1. Tracking adaptation-related development finance

The Intergovernmental Panel on Climate Change (IPCC) (2018[7]) defines adaptation as the process of adjustment of human and natural systems to actual and expected adverse effects of climate change, differentiating between incremental and transformational adaptation. Incremental adaptation "maintains the essence and integrity of a system or process at a given scale." Transformational adaptation "changes the fundamental attributes of a socio-ecological system in anticipation of climate change and its impacts." Continued incremental adaptation may accrue to transformational adaptation.

The adoption of the Paris Agreement raised the profile of climate change adaptation with the establishment of a global goal of "Enhancing adaptive capacity, strengthening resilience and reducing vulnerability to climate change, with a view to contributing to sustainable development and ensuring an adequate adaptation response in the context of the temperature goal referred to in Article 2" (Article 7.1). The Agreement further recognises that adaptation is a global challenge faced by all with local, subnational, national, regional and international dimensions (Article 7.2). Potential areas of collaboration for adaptation are elaborated in Article 7.7 and potential areas of focus in Article 7.9. This is complemented by a call for scaled-up financial resources to aim for a balance between adaptation and mitigation (Article 9.4). Further, the Agreement includes the establishment of adaptation communications as a means for countries to highlight their adaptation priorities, implementation and support needs, plans and actions (Article 7.10) (UNFCCC, 2015[8]).

Outside of the UNFCCC processes, the OECD Rio markers (OECD DAC, 2016[9]) and the joint MDB methodology for tracking climate finance (MDBs, 2020[10]) recommend a three-step approach for identifying adaptation-related finance (Table 1.1). While the two reporting frameworks are independent, the OECD eligibility criteria were informed by the already established joint MDB methodology when it underwent review and revision in 2015.

Table 1.1. Key steps of MDBs' and OECD Rio markers approach to track adaptation finance

MDB joint methodology	OECD DAC
Set out the climate-change vulnerability context of the project	Set out the context of risks, vulnerabilities, and impacts related to climate variability and climate change
Make an explicit statement of a project's intent to reduce climate vulnerability	State the intent to address the identified risks, vulnerabilities, and impacts in project documentation
Articulate a clear and direct link between specific project activities and the project's objective of reducing vulnerability to climate change.	Demonstrate a clear and direct link between the identified risks, vulnerabilities, and impacts and the specific project activities

Source: (MDBs, 2020[10]), (OECD DAC, 2016[9]).

The OECD Rio markers differentiate between commitments that include adaptation as a principal (or primary) objectives or as a significant (or secondary) objective. The full amount of commitments marked either principal or significant is reported in the OECD Creditor Reporting System (CRS). Many OECD members draw on the Rio-marked data when reporting their climate finance to the UNFCCC. In doing some, most adjust the amount reported, notably by applying coefficients (also see Annex B). The MDBs use a component approach which means that for each individual commitment an assessment is made to the determine the component focused on adaptation objectives and only that component is reported as adaptation, in their own reporting systems but also in the OECD CRS.

1.3. Instrument split

Over the period 2013-2018, the growth of public climate finance provided by developed countries (bilateral and multilateral attributed combined, excluding export credits) was mainly driven by developmental loans (Figure 1.3). Loans more than doubled from USD 19.8 billion in 2013 to USD 46.3 billion in 2018. After an initial fluctuation around USD 10 billion in 2013-15, grant financing grew to USD 12 billion in 2016 and retained similar values in the next two years. Equity appears as a marginal instrument during the six-year period, oscillating around USD 1 billion. In relative terms, the share of loans in public climate finance rose from 52% in 2013 to 74% in 2018 while the share of grants decreased from 27% in 2013 to 20% in 2018.

Figure 1.3. Public climate finance provided per instrument (2013-18, USD billion)

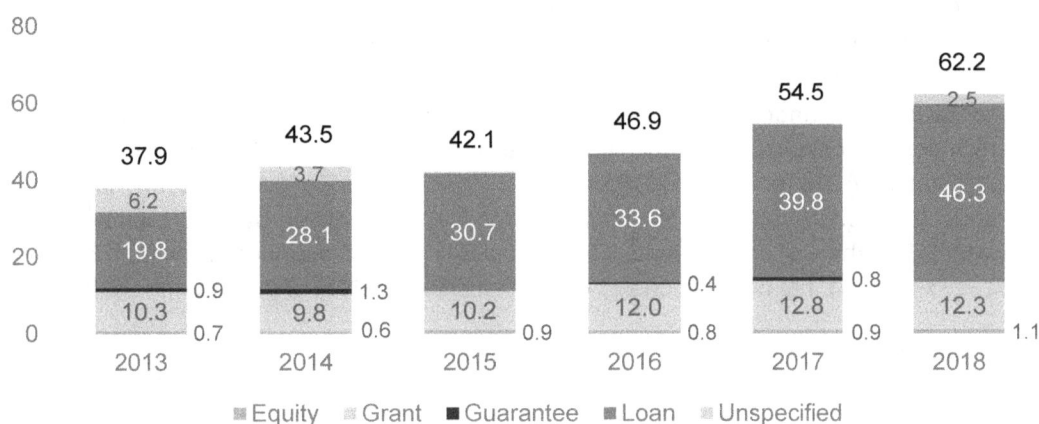

Note: Figures exclude export credits and mobilised private finance. Guarantees relate specifically to United States bilateral climate finance data, which includes developmental guarantees. For other bilateral providers and multilateral institutions, developmental guarantees are instead accounted for their mobilisation effect on private finance.
Source: based on Biennial Reports to the UNFCCC, OECD Development Assistance Committee statistics, as well as complementary reporting to the OECD.

As highlighted by previous OECD analyses (OECD, 2019[1]) and illustrated in Box 1.2, a majority (72%) of bilateral loans provided during 2016-18 were concessional according to ODA-related criteria. Multilateral providers do not extend concessional finance based on ODA-related considerations but rather on the income group status of the recipient. On that basis, 54% of loans committed by multilateral climate funds were reported as concessional. In contrast, the majority (76%) of MDB loans were labelled as non-concessional since they are for a large share provided to recipients outside the low-income countries (LICs) category. In practice, such non-concessional multilateral loans still present favourable terms and conditions compared to the capital market and/or are provided for activities in which the private sector may be reluctant to participate.

Breaking down the use of different public finance instruments by climate focus (Figure 1.6), equity investments and loans predominantly targeted mitigation objectives (89% and 75% respectively). In contrast, grants focused on adaptation and cross-cutting activities (38% and 29% respectively). The climate theme composition of grant and equity public finance was stable over the three years, in relative terms. On the other hand, the use of loans for adaptation increased from 16% in 2016 to 24% in 2018, while the share of loans for mitigation finance decreased from 79% in 2016 to 70% in 2018.

Box 1.2. Concessionality of loans: elements of definitions and illustrations

A concessional loan is extended to a borrower on more preferential terms than those available on the market. Such preferential terms may include below-market interest rates, extended grace periods, or a combination of both. Concessionality is an essential part of development finance. The reporting of concessional and non-concessional loans is, however, underpinned by different definitions for DAC members (bilateral donors and the EU) on the one hand and for multilateral development banks (MDBs) and other lending multilateral institutions on the other.

Concessionality of loans for DAC members

For DAC members, the level of concessionality of a loan is a core criterion for its eligibility to qualify as ODA. Concessionality is assessed through the "grant element" calculation, i.e. an assessment of the financial terms that takes into account four factors: the interest rate, the grace period, the maturity, and the discount rate. A loan is considered concessional if its grant element is above 10% for UMICs, 15% for LMICs or 45% for LDCs and other LICs. Furthermore, loans whose terms are not consistent with the IMF Debt Limits Policy or the World Bank's Non-Concessional Borrowing Policy are not reportable as ODA. Development finance loans that do not qualify as ODA are recorded as Other Official Flows (OOF). On that basis, and as highlighted in Figure 1.4, almost three-quarters (72%) of climate finance loans committed by DAC members in 2016-18 were concessional. The share of concessional loans committed by DAC members grew from 65% in 2016 to 80% in 2018 (+15%), noting that concessionality was unspecified for 20% of DAC members' loans in 2016.

Figure 1.4. Bilateral climate finance loans by concessionality level, (2016-18, %)

Source: based on Biennial Report to the UNFCCC.

Concessionality of multilateral loans

For lending by multilateral organisations (i.e. MDBs and multilateral climate funds), concessionality does not relate to a grant-element calculation, but rather to their ability to extend credit on financially-sustainable terms, based on their own financing costs. Multilateral concessional loans require external grant resources to be financially sustainable. Non-concessional loans are financially sustainable solely based on multilateral organisations' low cost of funding and preferred creditor status. Non-concessional multilateral loans may, therefore, be extended on more preferential terms than those available on the market terms. The use of concessional or non-concessional loans by multilateral organisations depends on the recipient country's income level as well as considerations for its creditworthiness and debt sustainability. In general, MICs and HICs can access non-concessional multilateral loans. On that basis, as highlighted in Figure 1.5 over three-quarters (77%) of MDB loans committed in 2016-18 were reported as non-concessional. On the other hand, 54% of loans extended by multilateral climate funds over the same period were reported as concessional.

Figure 1.5. Multilateral climate finance loans by concessionality level (2016-18, %)

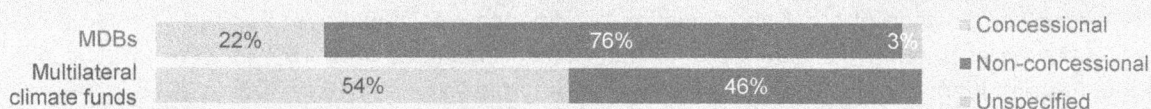

Source: based on OECD Development Assistance Committee statistics.

Figure 1.6. Public climate finance provided by climate focus and instrument (2016-18, %)

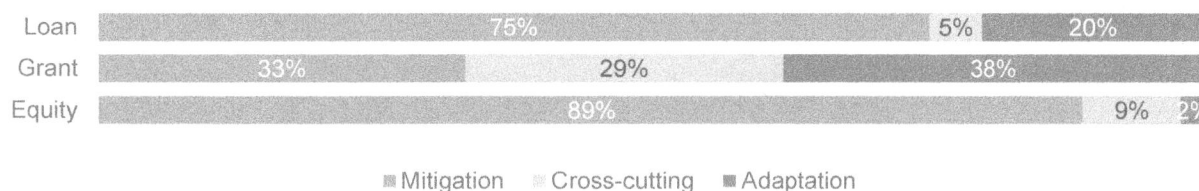

	Mitigation	Cross-cutting	Adaptation
Loan	75%	5%	20%
Grant	33%	29%	38%
Equity	89%	9%	2%

■ Mitigation ▦ Cross-cutting ■ Adaptation

Source: Based on Biennial Reports to the UNFCCC, OECD Development Assistance Committee statistics, as well as complementary reporting to the OECD.

Over 2016-18, the majority of climate-related export credits (72%) were provided in the form of credit risk guarantees to the lender against non-repayment by the borrower, while export credit loans represented (24%). For the remaining 4%, the instrument was unspecified. Data on private climate finance mobilised do not currently allow for an analysis by financial instrument as this information has not been collected thus far. Chapter 3, however, provides insights about the types of public finance mechanisms used by developed countries to mobilise private climate finance.

1.4. By sector

The energy sector, followed by the transport and storage sector were the most targeted sectors in the context of total climate finance provided and mobilised by developed countries in 2016-18 (Figure 1.7). With a yearly average of USD 23.8 billion, climate finance provided and mobilised towards energy accounted for 34% of the three-year average, followed by transport and storage (USD 9.7 billion; 14%), agriculture, forestry and fishing (USD 6 billion; 9%), water and sanitation (USD 5.2 billion; 7%) and banking and business services (USD 3.4 billion; 5%). Climate finance provided and mobilised for other sectors amounted to USD 13.4 billion (19%) per year on average during the three-year period, mainly including general environmental protection, health, education, other social infrastructure and multisector. The beneficiary sector was unspecified for the remaining 11% (USD 7.9 billion) of the three-year average.

Figure 1.7. Sectoral breakdown of climate finance provided and mobilised (2016-2018, %)

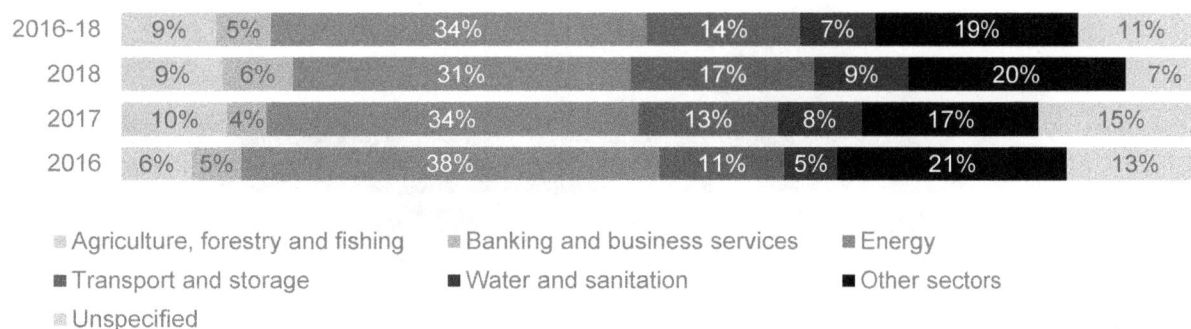

	Agriculture, forestry and fishing	Banking and business services	Energy	Transport and storage	Water and sanitation	Other sectors	Unspecified
2016-18	9%	5%	34%	14%	7%	19%	11%
2018	9%	6%	31%	17%	9%	20%	7%
2017	10%	4%	34%	13%	8%	17%	15%
2016	6%	5%	38%	11%	5%	21%	13%

▦ Agriculture, forestry and fishing ▦ Banking and business services ■ Energy
■ Transport and storage ■ Water and sanitation ■ Other sectors
▦ Unspecified

Source: based on Biennial Reports to the UNFCCC, OECD Development Assistance Committee statistics, OECD Export Credit Group statistics, as well as complementary reporting to the OECD.

Breaking down climate finance provided and mobilised in different sectors by climate focus (Figure 1.8), mitigation finance is clearly dominant in the energy (96%) and transport and storage (88%) sectors, as well as in the industry, mining and construction sectors (82%) and banking and business services (79%). In contrast, adaptation finance represented the largest share in water and sanitation (63%), agriculture, forestry and fishing (52%) and other social infrastructure (44%). The sectors where cross-cutting finance played a significant included general environment protection (39%), agriculture, forestry and fishing (20%) and multisector (17%).

Figure 1.8. Climate focus of climate finance provided and mobilised by sector (2016-18, %)

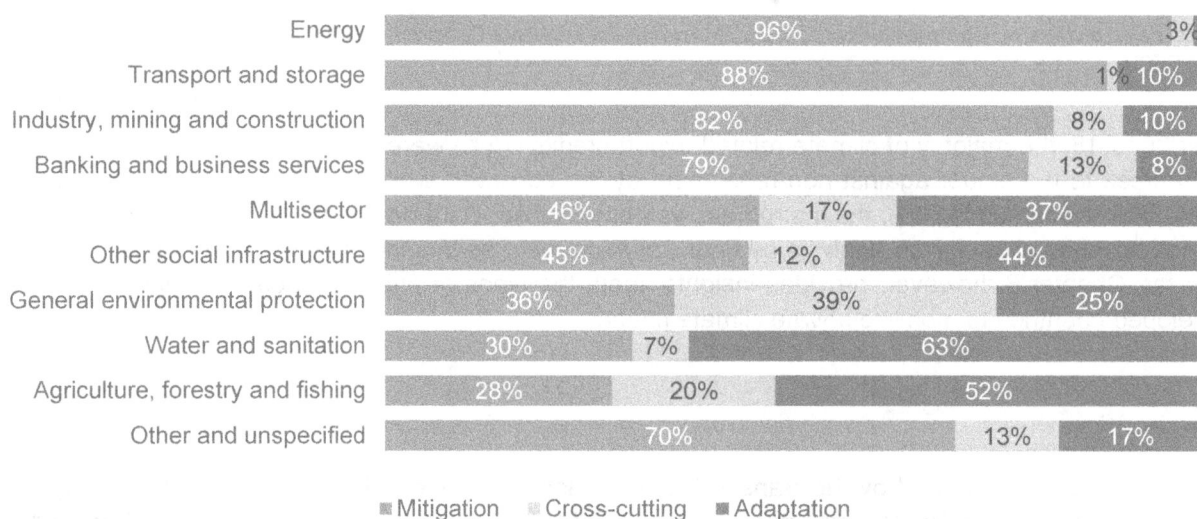

Sector	Mitigation	Cross-cutting	Adaptation
Energy	96%		3%
Transport and storage	88%	1%	10%
Industry, mining and construction	82%	8%	10%
Banking and business services	79%	13%	8%
Multisector	46%	17%	37%
Other social infrastructure	45%	12%	44%
General environmental protection	36%	39%	25%
Water and sanitation	30%	7%	63%
Agriculture, forestry and fishing	28%	20%	52%
Other and unspecified	70%	13%	17%

■ Mitigation   ■ Cross-cutting   ■ Adaptation

Source: based on Biennial Reports to the UNFCCC, OECD Development Assistance Committee statistics, OECD Export Credit Group statistics, as well as complementary reporting to the OECD.

Focusing on the sectoral breakdown in individual climate themes (Figure 1.9), almost two-thirds of climate finance provided and mobilised for mitigation during 2016-18 was primarily distributed over the energy (46%) and transport and storage sectors (17%). Around half adaptation finance provided and mobilised for the water and sanitation (24%) and the agriculture, forestry and fishing (23%) sectors, with 35% distributed over other sectors, including the broad category of general environmental protection and multisector as well as health, education and other social sectors.

Figure 1.9. Sectoral distribution of climate finance provided and mobilised by focus (2016-18, %)

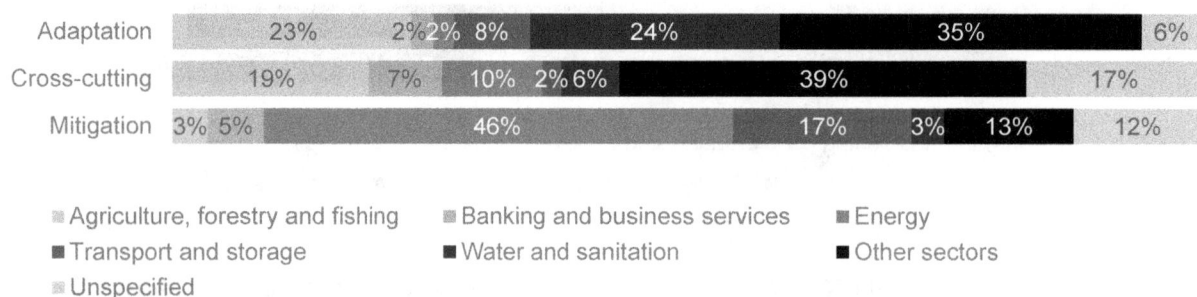

Focus	Agriculture, forestry and fishing	Banking and business services	Energy	Transport and storage	Water and sanitation	Other sectors	Unspecified
Adaptation	23%	2%	2%	8%	24%	35%	6%
Cross-cutting	19%	7%	10%	2% 6%	39%		17%
Mitigation	3% 5%		46%	17%	3%	13%	12%

■ Agriculture, forestry and fishing   ■ Banking and business services   ■ Energy
■ Transport and storage   ■ Water and sanitation   ■ Other sectors
■ Unspecified

Source: based on Biennial Reports to the UNFCCC, OECD Development Assistance Committee statistics, OECD Export Credit Group statistics, as well as complementary reporting to the OECD.

Box 1.3. Focus on climate finance in the energy sector

The energy sector represented 34% of total climate finance provided and mobilised by developed countries over 2016-18, the highest share among all sectors. This represented USD 23.8 billion per year on average, out of which:

- USD 12.5 billion (53%) targeted projects for energy generation from renewable sources, particularly solar, wind, and hydropower;
- USD 1.2 billion (5%), targeted energy generation from selected non-renewable sources, mainly including natural gas-fired, hybrid, and waste-fired electric power plants. Coal-related finance is excluded altogether from these and earlier volumes;
- USD 2.2 billion (9%) was allocated to energy distribution (both electricity and gas);
- USD 7.8 billion (33%) related to energy policy, efficiency, or unspecified activities in the energy sector (referred to as 'energy, general').

Figure 1.10. Breakdown of climate finance provided and mobilised in the energy sector (2016-2018, %)

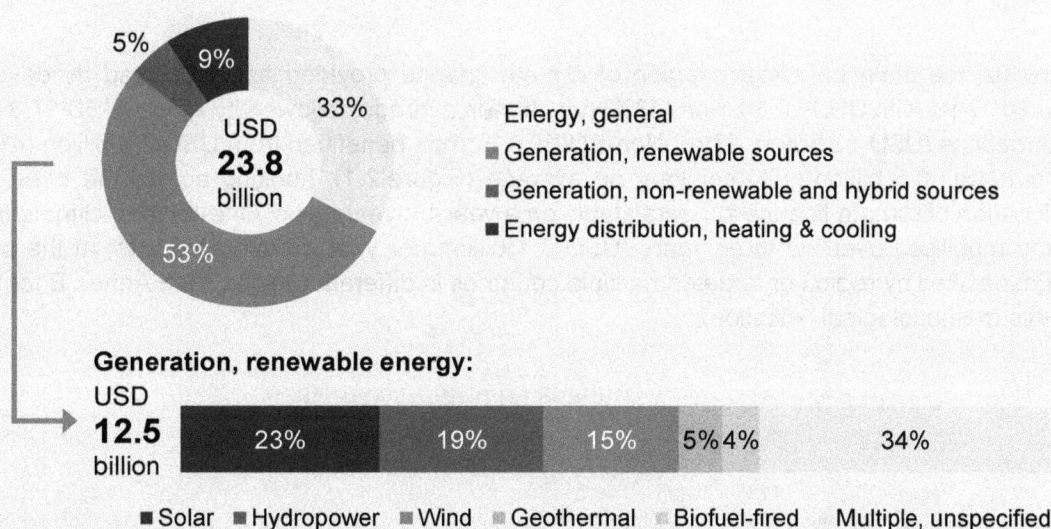

Source: based on Biennial Reports to the UNFCCC, OECD Development Assistance Committee statistics, OECD Export Credit Group statistics, as well as complementary reporting to the OECD.

Out of the USD 23.8 billion per year on average, 61% consisted of public climate finance from bilateral and multilateral providers, mostly in the form of loans (84% of public finance provided) and to a lesser extent grants (13%) and equity investments (2%). A further 33% of total energy-related climate finance was mobilised from the private sector and the remaining 6% related to officially supported export credits. Overall, 96% of energy-related climate finance targeted climate change mitigation. The shares of loans, mobilised private finance and mitigation in the energy sector are significantly higher than for all sectors.

Asia benefitted from the highest portion (46%) of energy-related climate finance. This is mainly driven by large sums allocated to South Asia and East Asia. Africa and the Americas represented approximately a quarter each (26% and 22% respectively).

2 Geographical breakdown

This chapter provides an analysis of climate finance provided and mobilised by developed countries for developing countries broken down by regions[1], recipient countries, and country income groups. The analysis includes views on distribution by total volume as well as per capita. Annex C provides a full list of recipient countries and territories considered in this report.

2.1. By region

Asia was by far the main beneficiary region of climate finance provided and mobilised by developed countries in 2016-18, with USD 30.1 billion (43%) per year on average, followed by Africa (USD 17.3 billion; 25%) and Americas (USD 12 billion; 17%). Non-EU/EEA Europe benefitted from USD 2.4 billion (4%) and Oceania from USD 0.5 billion (1%) per year on average (Figure 2.1). Looking across the three years, regional allocation of climate finance appears stable on a year-by-year basis. One-tenth of climate finance provided and mobilised over the three years (USD 7.1 billion per year on average) was, at the point of reporting, unspecified by region or targeted multiple countries in different regions (See Annex B for further details on this methodological limitation).

Figure 2.1. Climate finance provided and mobilised by region (2016-18, %)

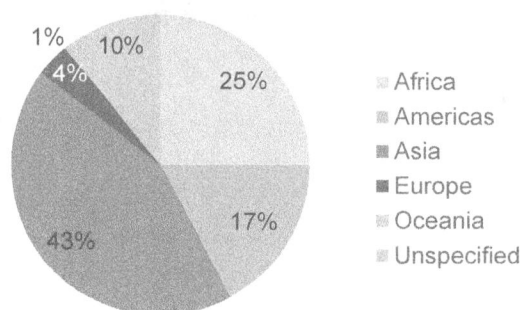

Note: The regions cover only developing countries as defined in Annex C.
Source: Based on Biennial Reports to the UNFCCC, OECD Development Assistance Committee statistics, OECD Export Credit Group statistics, as well as complementary reporting to the OECD.

At a sub-regional level (Figure 2.2), it can be observed that during 2016-18:

- In Asia, climate finance mostly targeted South Asia (USD 12.5 billion; 18% of total climate finance per year on average) and East Asia (USD 9.1 billion; 13%). Central Asia (USD 1.9 billion; 3%).

- In Africa, climate finance was predominantly allocated to Eastern (USD 4.8 billion; 7%), Northern (USD 4.1 billion, 6%), and Western Africa (USD 3.3. billion; 5%). Central Africa (USD 1.1. billion) and Southern Africa (USD 0.8 billion) benefitted from 3% combined.

- In Americas, climate finance was mainly directed to South America (USD 8.5 billion; 12%), followed by Central America (USD 2.3 billion; 3%) and the Caribbean (USD 0.7 billion; 1%).

Figure 2.2. Climate finance provided and mobilised by sub-region (2016-18, USD billion annual average, %)

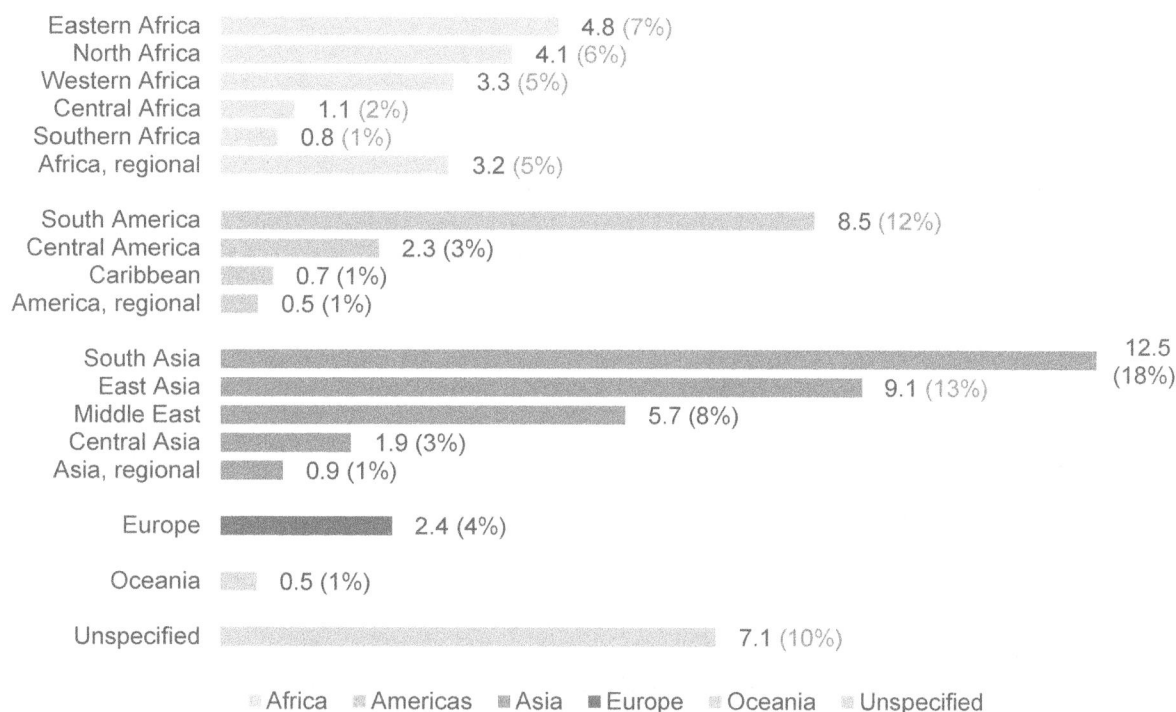

Note: The regions cover only developing countries as defined in Annex C.
Source: Based on Biennial Reports to the UNFCCC, OECD Development Assistance Committee statistics, OECD Export Credit Group statistics, as well as complementary reporting to the OECD.

Regions and sub-regions with relatively low populations benefitted from the highest amounts of climate finance per capita over 2016-18 (Figure 2.3), especially in the case for Oceania (USD 47 per capita for a population of 11 million), developing countries in Europe (USD 31.3 per capita for a population of 78 million), and the Central Asia sub-region (USD 21.2 per capita for a population of 88 million). Other sub-regions with high per capita receipts include Northern Africa (USD 21.6 for a population of 192 million) and South America (USD 20.2 for a population of 419 million).

In contrast, highly populated regions, especially East Asia (population of 2.1 billion) and South Asia (population of 1.9 billion), were allocated the lowest amounts per capita (USD 4.3 and 6.8, respectively) per year on average during 2016-18. Sub-Sahara Africa, in its entirety (population 1.1 billion) benefitted from USD 9.5 per capita but with significant variations at a sub-regional level. For example, Southern Africa (population of 64.8 million) received USD 12.5 per capita, whereas Central Africa (population of 164 million) only USD 6.4 per capita.

Figure 2.3. Climate finance provided and mobilised per capita by sub-region (2016-18, USD annual average)

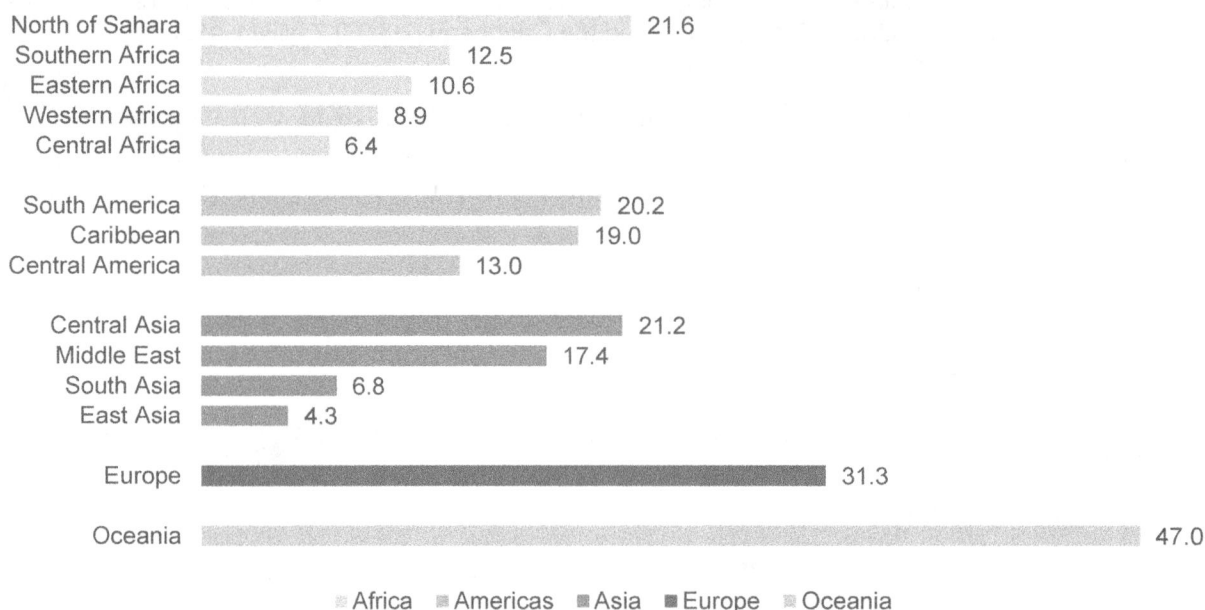

North of Sahara	21.6
Southern Africa	12.5
Eastern Africa	10.6
Western Africa	8.9
Central Africa	6.4
South America	20.2
Caribbean	19.0
Central America	13.0
Central Asia	21.2
Middle East	17.4
South Asia	6.8
East Asia	4.3
Europe	31.3
Oceania	47.0

Africa Americas Asia Europe Oceania

Note: The regions cover only developing countries as defined in Annex C.
Source: based on Biennial Reports to the UNFCCC, OECD Development Assistance Committee statistics, OECD Export Credit Group statistics, as well as complementary reporting to the OECD. Population data: (UN DESA, 2019[11]) complemented with (EUROSTAT, 2019[12]).

2.2. By income group

Over 2016-18, on average per year, out of the USD 55.2 billion was allocable by country (79% of the annual average climate finance total). The remaining USD 14.3 billion (21%) was reported as having a broader, regional scope, and could therefore not be allocated by income group.

As illustrated in Figure 2.4, middle-income countries were the primary recipients of climate finance in 2016-18. On on average per year USD 28.1 billion (40% of the total) targeted lower-middle-income countries (LMICs) and USD 19.9 billion (29%) upper-middle-income countries (UMICs). Low-income countries (LICs) accounted for USD 5.4 billion (8%). High-income countries (HICs) within the scope of "developing countries" considered in the analysis (see Annex C) accounted for USD 1.7 billion (2%). Further, Figure 2.4 illustrates a difference in focus between the different components that underpin the figures. While bilateral public climate finance strongly focused on LMICs, multilateral public climate finance and mobilised private finance are more evenly spread between LMICs and UMICs.

Figure 2.4. Climate finance provided and mobilised according to recipient country income group (2016-18 average, USD billion)

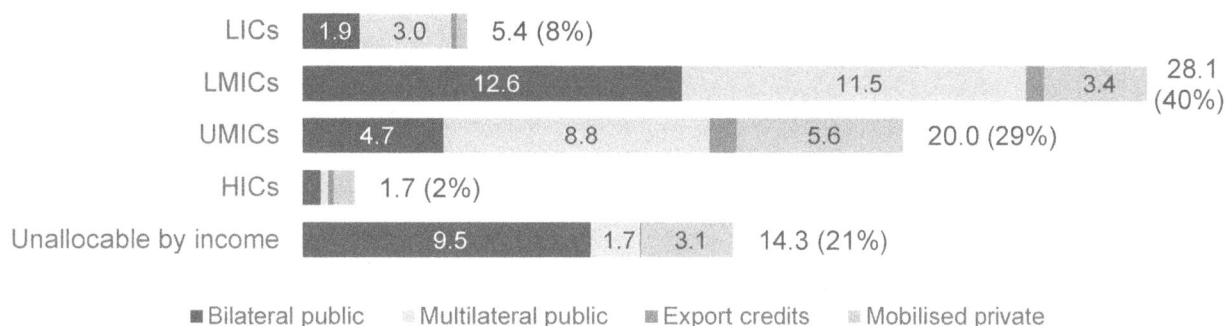

LICs 1.9 3.0 5.4 (8%)
LMICs 12.6 11.5 3.4 28.1 (40%)
UMICs 4.7 8.8 5.6 20.0 (29%)
HICs 1.7 (2%)
Unallocable by income 9.5 1.7 3.1 14.3 (21%)

■ Bilateral public ▨ Multilateral public ▨ Export credits ▨ Mobilised private

Source: Based on Biennial Reports to the UNFCCC, OECD Development Assistance Committee statistics, OECD Export Credit Group statistics, as well as complementary reporting to the OECD. For income groups: (World Bank, 2020[13]), complemented with (OECD, 2020[14]) for territories not classified by the World Bank.

The climate focus of total climate finance provided and mobilised within individual income groups was fairly stable over the three years. Figure 2.5 shows that the higher the recipient country income level, the higher the share of climate finance targeting mitigation, and the lower the share of climate finance targeting adaptation. Indeed, in 2016-18, 92% of finance allocated to the limited number of HICs considered within the scope of the analysis targeted mitigation; only 7% targeted adaptation objectives. In contrast, the shares of mitigation and adaptation finance for LICs were almost equal at 46% and 44%, respectively.

Figure 2.5. Climate finance provided and mobilised according to income group and focus (2016-18, %)

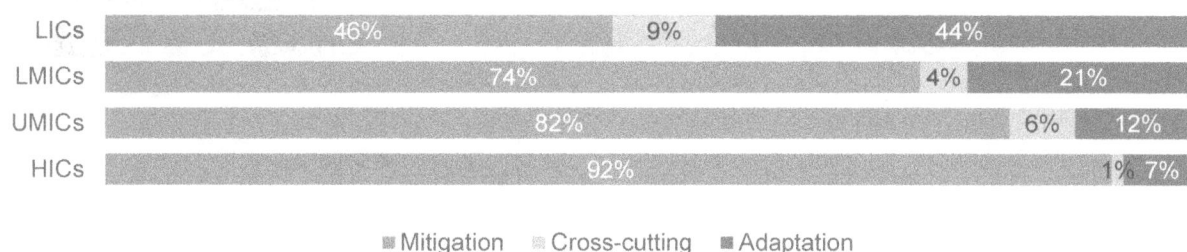

LICs 46% 9% 44%
LMICs 74% 4% 21%
UMICs 82% 6% 12%
HICs 92% 1% 7%

▨ Mitigation ▨ Cross-cutting ■ Adaptation

Note: Only climate finance allocated to individual developing countries (79% of the total over 2016-18) is included in this chart.
Source: Based on Biennial Reports to the UNFCCC, OECD Development Assistance Committee statistics, OECD Export Credit Group statistics, as well as complementary reporting to the OECD. For income groups: (World Bank, 2020[13]), complemented with (OECD, 2020[14]) for territories not classified by the World Bank.

A correlation can also be observed between financial instruments and income group in the context of public bilateral and multilateral public finance (Figure 2.6). The higher the income of the recipient country, the lower the share of grants, and the higher the share of loans. While developed country public finance for the HICs was clearly dominated by loans (96%), grants played the most important role in the LICs (42%). In MICs, most of public climate finance was provided through loans (88% in UMICs and 89% in LMICs), while grants accounted for 10% in both groups. Equity investments were mostly used in UMICs (1.4%).

Figure 2.6. Public climate finance according to income group and instrument (2016-18, %)

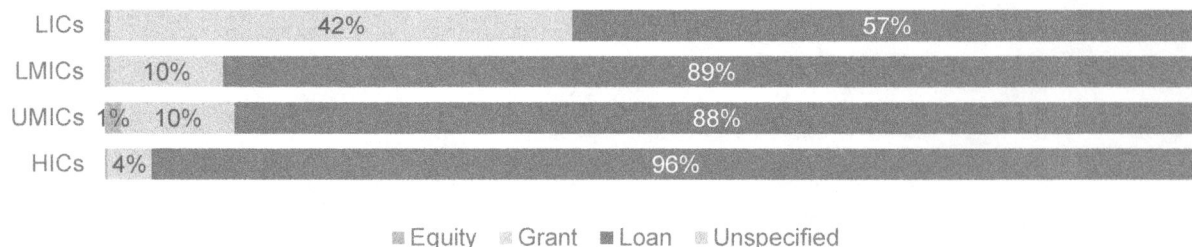

LICs	42%	57%
LMICs	10%	89%
UMICs	1% 10%	88%
HICs	4%	96%

■ Equity ▨ Grant ■ Loan ▨ Unspecified

Note: Only climate finance allocated to individual developing countries (79% of the total over 2016-18) is included in this chart.
Source: Based on Biennial Reports to the UNFCCC, OECD Development Assistance Committee statistics, OECD Export Credit Group statistics, as well as complementary reporting to the OECD. For income groups: (World Bank, 2020[13]), complemented with (OECD, 2020[14]) for territories not classified by the World.

Regarding the sectoral distribution of climate finance provided and mobilised by developed countries for developing countries in 2016-18 (Figure 2.7), energy was the largest sector across all income groups. Its share, however, increased significantly with income level, from 34% in LICs to 75% in HICs. Agriculture, forestry and fishing were targeted to the greatest extent in LICs (18%) and LMICs (11%) but almost not in UMICs (4%) and HICs (1%). Transport and storage benefitted from the largest share in LMICs (25%). Water and sanitation reached about 10% across LICs, LMICs and HICs.

Figure 2.7. Climate finance according to income group and sector (2016-18, %)

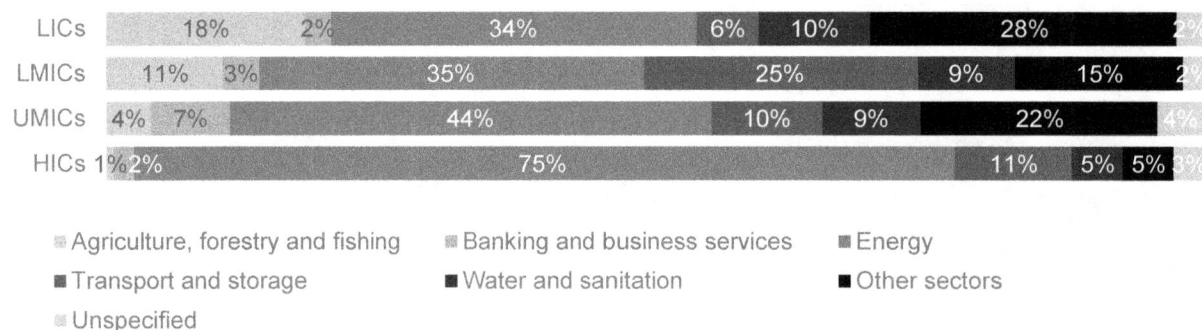

LICs	18%	2%	34%	6% 10%	28%	2%
LMICs	11%	3%	35%	25%	9% 15%	2%
UMICs	4% 7%	44%	10% 9%	22%	4%
HICs	1% 2%	75%	11% 5% 5%	3%

▨ Agriculture, forestry and fishing   ▨ Banking and business services   ■ Energy
■ Transport and storage   ■ Water and sanitation   ■ Other sectors
▨ Unspecified

Note: Only climate finance allocated to individual developing countries (79% of the total over 2016-18) is included in this chart.
Source: Based on Biennial Reports to the UNFCCC, OECD Development Assistance Committee statistics, OECD Export Credit Group statistics, as well as complementary reporting to the OECD. For income groups: (World Bank, 2020[13]), complemented with (OECD, 2020[14]) for territories not classified by the World Bank.

2.3. By country

Many large and highly populated middle-income developing countries were the primary beneficiaries of climate finance provided and mobilised in 2016-18 (Figure 2.8). Further, all developing countries which benefitted from climate finance of over USD 1 billion per year on average in 2016-18 were MICs (LMICs or UMICs). The average yearly amounts by individual MICs varied considerably, whereas most LICs were allocated an average of USD 50-300 million per year. Most SIDS (see Box 2.1) and HICs benefitted from the lowest amounts of climate finance (see also Figure 2.10).

Figure 2.8. Climate finance provided and mobilised per recipient country (2016 18 average, USD billion)

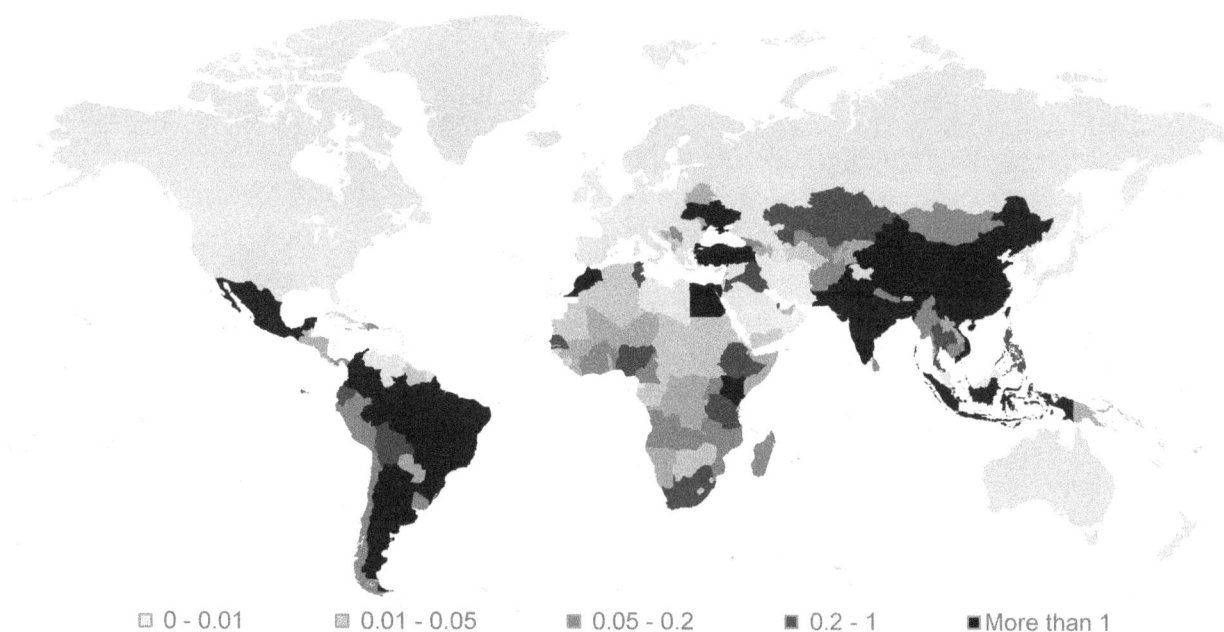

□ 0 - 0.01   ▨ 0.01 - 0.05   ▣ 0.05 - 0.2   ▨ 0.2 - 1   ■ More than 1

Note: Only climate finance allocated to individual developing countries (79% of the total over 2016-18) is included in this visual. Climate finance not allocable by country amounted to a USD 14.3 billion per year on average over 2016-18.
Source: Based on Biennial Reports to the UNFCCC, OECD Development Assistance Committee statistics, OECD Export Credit Group statistics, as well as complementary reporting to the OECD. Population data: (UN DESA, 2019[11]) complemented with (EUROSTAT, 2019[12]).

An analysis by country per capita of climate finance provided and mobilised in 2016-18 offers a different picture. Typically, countries and territories with the highest receipts per capita included SIDS and countries with a relatively low population (Figure 2.9 and Figure 2.10). Twenty-one of the top 25 recipients per capita included SIDS in Oceania, the Caribbean, and Africa. The remaining four recipients are countries with less than 10 million inhabitants. These top 25 countries and territories benefitted from more than USD 69 per capita per year on average. In contrast, LICs received, on average, less than USD 15 per capita. Countries and territories with the lowest per capita receipts included HICs primarily in the Middle East and conflict-affected MICs and LICs.

Considering adaptation and mitigation finance separately, the following insights can be drawn:

- The main per capita beneficiaries of adaptation finance remain SIDS and countries with a population below 10 million. The list of top 20 adaptation finance recipients per capita includes 18 SIDS, all of which were allocated over USD 25 per capita of adaptation finance. Further, 42 of top 50 recipients of adaptation climate finance per capita were countries with a population below 10 million, six with a population of 10-20 million and two with a population above 20 million.

- The main per capita recipients of mitigation finance included a wider range of countries. While over half of the top 20 per capita beneficiaries of mitigation finance were SIDS, the list also included seven other countries with a population below 10 million. In contrast to adaptation finance, the list of top 50 per capita recipients of mitigation finance included 13 countries of a population above 10 million, five of which above 40 million.

Figure 2.9. Climate finance provided and mobilised per capita by country (2016-18 average, USD)

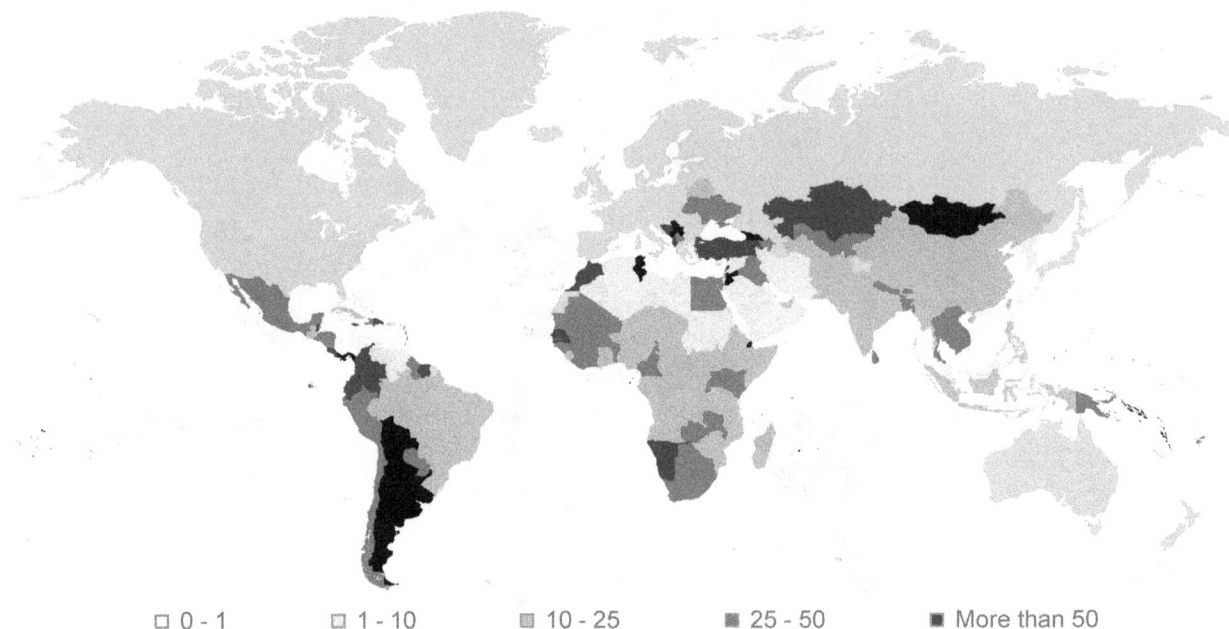

□ 0 - 1   □ 1 - 10   ▦ 10 - 25   ■ 25 - 50   ■ More than 50

Note: Only climate finance allocated to individual a countries (79% of the total over 2016-18) is included in this visual.
Source: based on Biennial Reports to the UNFCCC, OECD Development Assistance Committee statistics, OECD Export Credit Group statistics, as well as complementary reporting to the OECD. Population data: (UN DESA, 2019[11]) complemented with (EUROSTAT, 2019[12]).

In addition, Figure 2.10 displays climate finance provided and mobilised by developed countries for individual developing countries and territories (anonymised) per year on average during 2016-18, organised by income level. SIDS represent the majority of countries and territories with the lowest amounts of climate finance in absolute terms (primarily below USD 100 million), but the highest amounts on a per capita basis (mainly USD 100 and higher). Further, climate finance allocated to individual LDCs shows significant differences ranging between USD 10 million and USD 1 billion in absolute terms but was concentrated around USD 10 on a per capita basis. Overall, Figure 2.10 also suggests that the higher the income level of the recipient, the lower the amounts allocated. On a per-capita basis, a similar trend is less obvious to identify, although most MICs benefitted from between USD 10 to 100 per capita.

Figure 2.10. Climate finance by country per income level (2016-18 average)

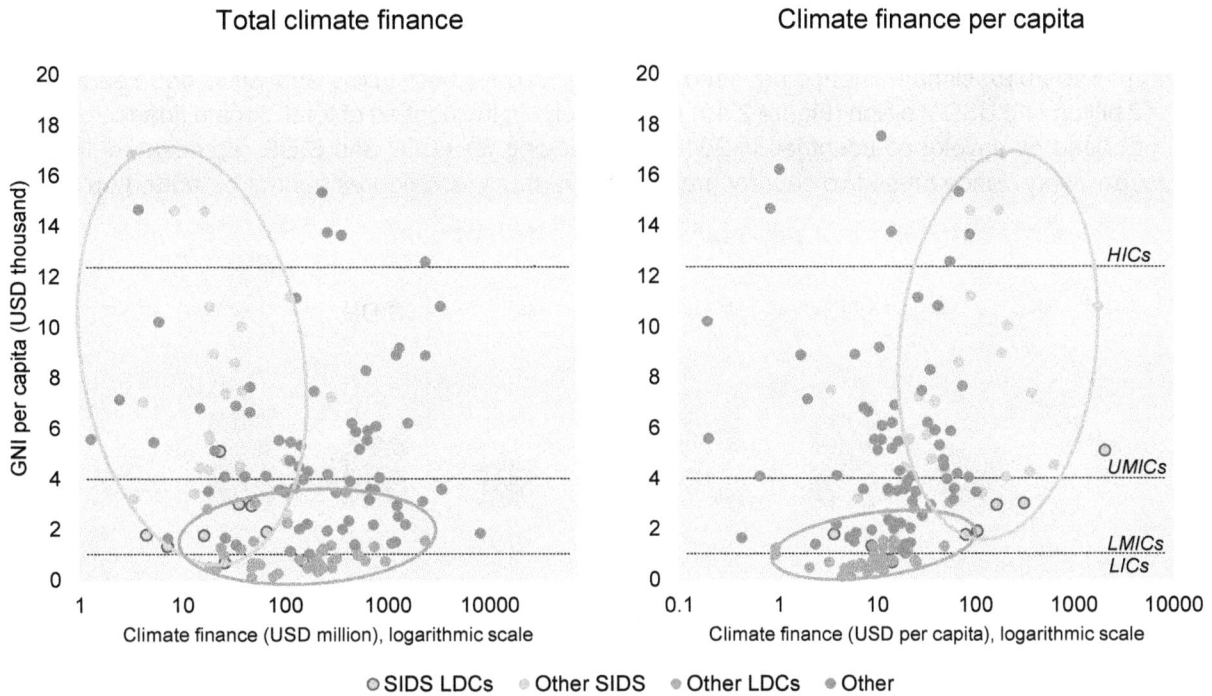

Total climate finance

Climate finance per capita

○ SIDS LDCs ○ Other SIDS ● Other LDCs ● Other

Note: Only climate finance allocated to individual developing countries (79% of the total over 2016-18) is included in this visual.
Source: Based on Biennial Reports to the UNFCCC, OECD Development Assistance Committee statistics, OECD Export Credit Group statistics, as well as complementary reporting to the OECD. GNI per capita data: World Bank.

Box 2.1. Climate finance to SIDS and LDCs

From 2016 to 2018, climate finance provided and mobilised for both LDCs and SIDS doubled to reach USD 12 billion and USD 2 billion (Figure 2.10) respectively. In the context of total climate finance provided and mobilised by developed countries in 2016-18, financing for LDCs and SIDS represented 14% and 2%, respectively. Since these two country groupings overlap, these figures cannot be added up.

Figure 2.11. Finance to SIDS and LDCs (2016-18, USD billion)

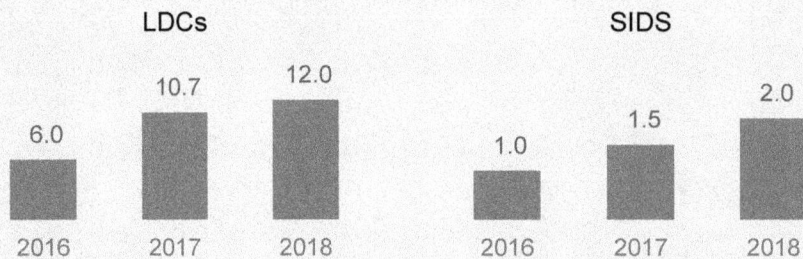

Source: Based on Biennial Reports to the UNFCCC, OECD Development Assistance Committee statistics, OECD Export Credit Group statistics, as well as complementary reporting to the OECD. For SIDS: (UN-OHRLLS, 2020[15]), for LDCs: (UN-OHRLLS, 2020[16]).

Climate finance for both LDCs and SIDS was focused on adaptation objectives (41% and 39% respectively). The share of grants in public climate finance for both groupings (49% for SIDS and 33% LDCs) was higher than the trends observed for climate finance provided and mobilised to all developing countries (19%).

Figure 2.12. Finance to SIDS and LDCs by climate focus and instrument, (2016-18, %)

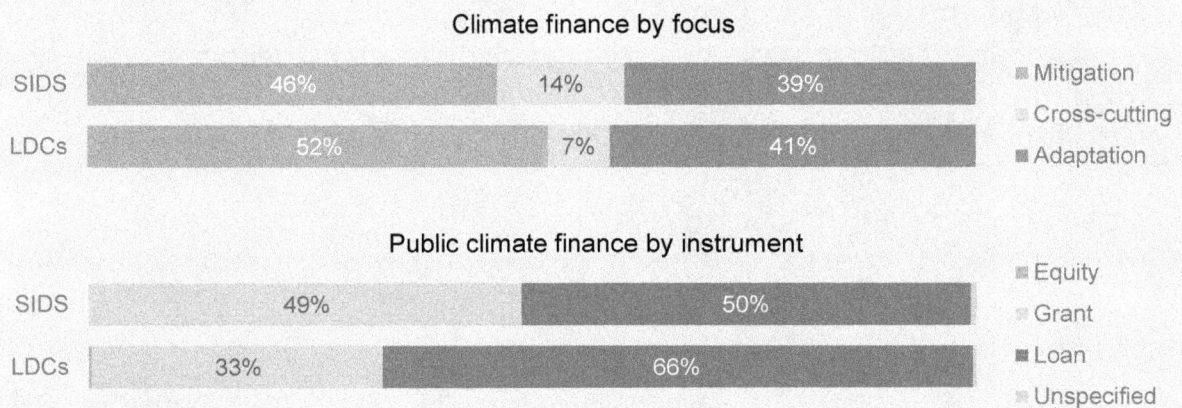

Source: Based on Biennial Reports to the UNFCCC, OECD Development Assistance Committee statistics, OECD Export Credit Group statistics, as well as complementary reporting to the OECD. For SIDS: (UN-OHRLLS, 2020[15]), For LDCs: (UN-OHRLLS, 2020[16]).

The proportion represented by the energy sector and transport and storage sector was somewhat lower in the LDCs and SIDS (45% and 41%) than for all developing countries (see Section 1.4), mainly in favour of water and sanitation and other social infrastructure, which together accounted for 13% in SIDS and 17% in LDCs. Agriculture, forestry and fishing accounted for 17% of climate finance provided and mobilised by developed countries for the LDCs and 11% for the SIDS.

3 Private climate finance mobilised

As further detailed in Annex B, the OECD has developed an international standard for measuring the amounts mobilised from the private sector by official development finance interventions, including for climate. Work has been carried out over multiple years and successive rounds of research, stakeholder consultations, surveys, methodological developments, and implementation. On that basis, this chapter analyses private-sector finance (typically in the form of market-term loans or equity) mobilised by bilateral or multilateral public finance interventions, e.g. by means of de-risking instruments. The measure of private finance mobilisation does not capture private finance invested in the absence of public finance interventions, e.g. private investment that may have been catalysed by domestic norms and fiscal policies or by upstream capacity building, or finance provided by private philanthropies (see Box 3.1).

The chapter analyses private climate finance mobilised by developed countries according to mechanisms, climate focus, sector, region and recipient countries' income groups. The chapter also offers insights on how such private climate finance compares to private finance mobilised for non-climate activities. The latter corresponds to private finance mobilised by bilateral and multilateral development finance providers that was reported to the OECD DAC without being marked as climate-related. For reasons explained earlier in this report, the analysis of mobilised private climate finance is limited to 2016-18.

3.1. Climate in total private finance mobilised

Total private finance mobilised attributed to developed countries (including climate and non-climate finance) remained stable in 2016 (USD 32.4 billion) and 2017 (USD 33.1 billion) and increased significantly to reach USD 42.6 billion in 2018 (a year-on-year increase of 29%).

Figure 3.1. Private finance mobilised for climate and non-climate activities attributed to developed countries (2016-18, USD billion)

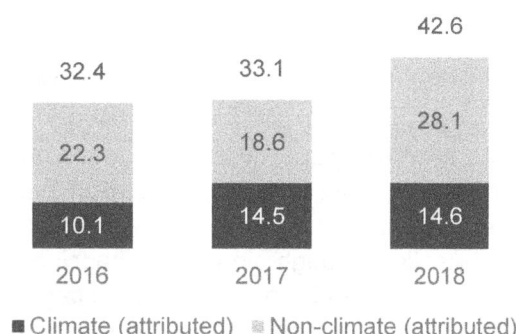

■ Climate (attributed)   ▨ Non-climate (attributed)

Note: For a limited number of providers, the data reported to the OECD did not include non-climate mobilised private finance. Consequently, total private finance mobilised by developed countries and, within that non-climate mobilised private finance may be partly underestimated.
Source: OECD Development Assistance Committee statistics as well as complementary reporting to the OECD.

As a subset of this total, private climate finance mobilised followed a different trend: it first grew from USD 10.1 billion in 2016 to USD 14.5 billion in 2017 (a year-on-year increase of 43%) and then remained stable in 2018 (USD 14.6 billion).

3.2. By mechanism to mobilise private finance

Activity-level data collected by the OECD on amounts mobilised from the private sector enable to distinguish between financial mechanisms used by official development finance providers to mobilise private finance. The OECD methodology for measuring mobilised private finance follows a mechanism approach. As such, it distinguishes between guarantees, syndicated loans, shares in collective investment vehicles (CIVs), direct investment in companies or special purpose vehicles (SPVs), credits lines and simple co-financing arrangements (see Annex B, as well as (OECD DAC, 2020[6]) and (OECD, 2019[11]) for further details). For confidentiality reasons, such data neither include information about the financial instrument used by the private sector, nor the financial terms relating to the private investment.

Over 2016-18, the majority of private climate finance was mobilised through direct investment in companies or SPVs (43%) guarantees (23%), syndicated loans (14%). The share of private climate finance mobilised through guarantees and syndicated more than doubled from 2016 to 2018 (from 15% to 31% and 7% to 19%, respectively). On the contrary, the share of private climate finance mobilised through direct investment in companies or SPVs dropped from 54% in 2016 to 33% in 2018. Further, the share of private climate finance mobilised through shares in CIVs, and simple co-financing remained relatively modest over the three-year period (4% and 6% respectively). Credit lines, which represented 13% in both 2016 and 2017, dropped significantly in 2018, accounting for 6% only.

Figure 3.2. Private climate finance mobilised by mechanism and year (2016-18, %)

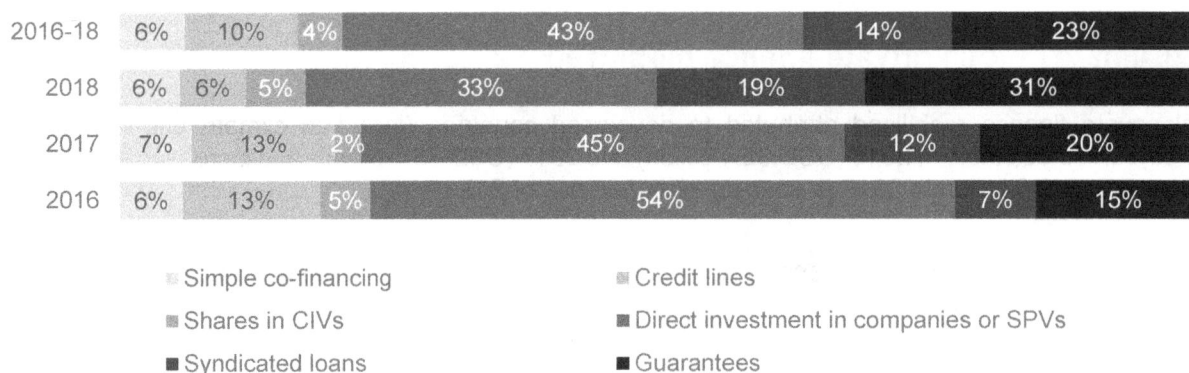

Source: OECD Development Assistance Committee statistics as well as complementary reporting to the OECD.

Figure 3.3 displays the share represented respectively by climate and non-climate private finance mobilised for each mobilisation mechanism. Over half (54%) of total private finance mobilised by developed countries in 2016-18 through direct investment in companies or SPVs were for climate. The share of climate in total private finance mobilisation through simple co-financing was 41% and syndicated loans 37%. These relatively high shares may relate to the fact that syndicated loans and direct investment in companies or SPVs are frequently used in the context of large infrastructure projects that often aim at climate objectives. In contrast, the share of private climate finance mobilised by developed countries in total private finance mobilised through credit lines, guarantees and shares in CIVs was significantly lower (27%, 26% and 20% respectively).

Figure 3.3. Private finance mobilised for climate and non-climate activities by mechanism (2016-18, %)

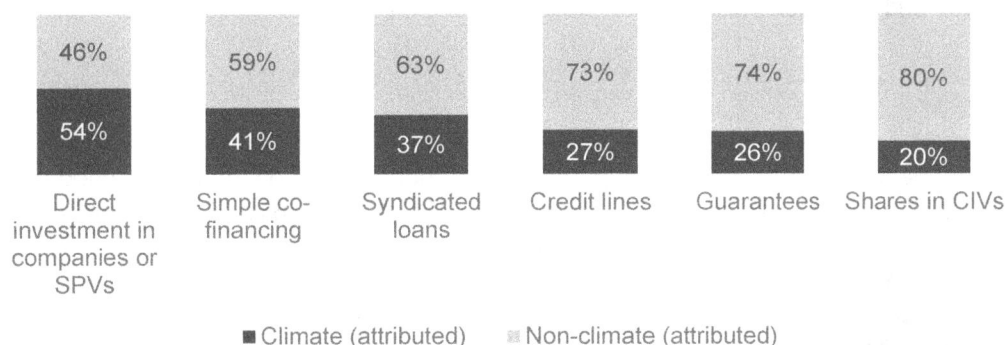

Note: For a limited number of providers, the data reported to the OECD did not include non-climate mobilised private finance. Consequently, total private finance mobilised by developed countries and, within that non-climate mobilised private finance may be partly underestimated.
Source: OECD Development Assistance Committee statistics as well as complementary reporting to the OECD.

The relatively lower shares represented by climate in total private finance mobilised through credit lines, guarantees and shares in CIVs may in part be due to difficulties in tracking climate-relevance. These instruments often target small and medium-sized enterprises via financial intermediaries (portfolio guarantees and credit lines) or pooling and other collective investment vehicles. Assessing the climate focus or relevance of downstream investments can be challenging due to the limited availability of information available at the point of the public finance intervention on the actual downstream use of the finance (also see sectoral analysis in Section 3.4).

In contrast, information on the climate focus of activities without an intermediary, such as direct investment in companies and SPVs, investment guarantees, syndicated loans for infrastructure projects, or simple co-financing arrangements, is typically available at the commitment stage of the public finance intervention.

3.3. By climate focus

Over 93% of private climate finance mobilised by developed countries over 2016-18 benefited mitigation (Figure 3.4). In contrast, adaptation and cross-cutting each accounted for 3% to 4%. The respective relative shares of mitigation, adaptation and cross-cutting were almost identical in each of the three years.

Figure 3.4. Private climate finance mobilised by climate focus and year (2016-18, %)

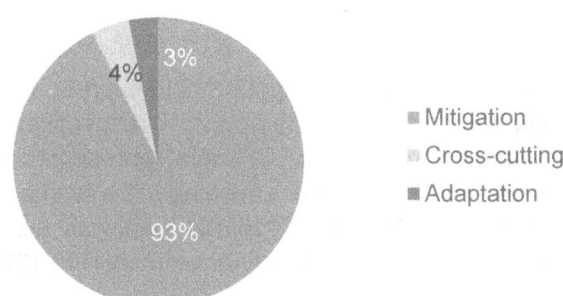

Source: OECD Development Assistance Committee statistics as well as complementary reporting to the OECD.

As highlighted in Box 1.1, methodologies to track adaptation finance differ from those to track mitigation finance. When it comes to mobilised private finance specifically, there likely remains room for improvement in identifying adaptation-relevant activities, for instance, in cases where climate resilience is mainstreamed into investments and business decisions.

3.4. By sector

Private climate finance mobilised by developed countries during 2016-18 mainly focused on the energy sector (USD 7.8 billion (60%) per year on average). Only USD 1 billion (6%) of private climate finance was mobilised in the industry, mining and construction sectors, followed by banking and business services (USD 0.9 billion; 7%), agriculture, forestry and fishing, and transport and storage (USD 0.4 billion; 3% each). In contrast, banking and business services was the main sector benefitting from non-climate private finance mobilised, with an annual average of USD 9.9 billion (42% of private non-climate finance mobilised by developing countries). These figures confirm the observation in Section 3.2 that a large share of non-climate mobilisation is mobilised via financial intermediaries, which may sometimes make it more difficult to assign private mobilisation to a specific sector or assess its potential climate relevance.

Figure 3.5. Private finance mobilised by sector and year (2016-18 average, USD billion)

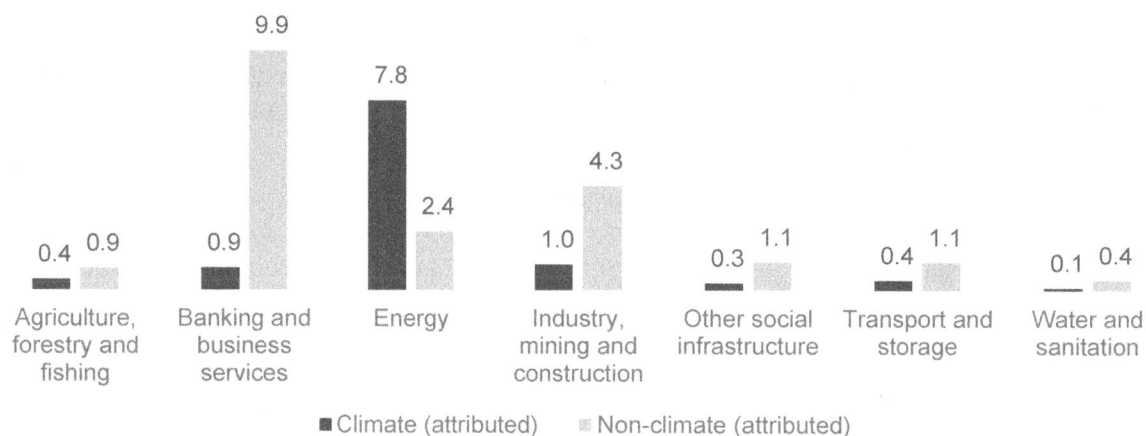

Note: For a limited number of providers, the data reported to the OECD did not include non-climate mobilised private finance. Consequently, total private finance mobilised by developed countries and, within that non-climate mobilised private finance may be partly underestimated.
Source: OECD Development Assistance Committee statistics as well as complementary reporting to the OECD.

3.5. By region

During 2016-18, as displayed in Figure 3.6, developed countries predominantly mobilised private climate finance for projects in Asia and the Americas (44% and 25% respectively). Africa represented 17% and Europe 4%. Private climate finance mobilised for Oceania represented 0.01% of total climate finance mobilised by developed countries (Figure 3.6). The remaining 9% was unspecified by region. In the context of non-climate private finance mobilised during 2016-18, Asia was also the main beneficiary region, although to a lesser extent than for climate private finance mobilised (32% of total non-climate private finance mobilised).

Figure 3.6. Private climate finance mobilised by region and year (2016-18, %)

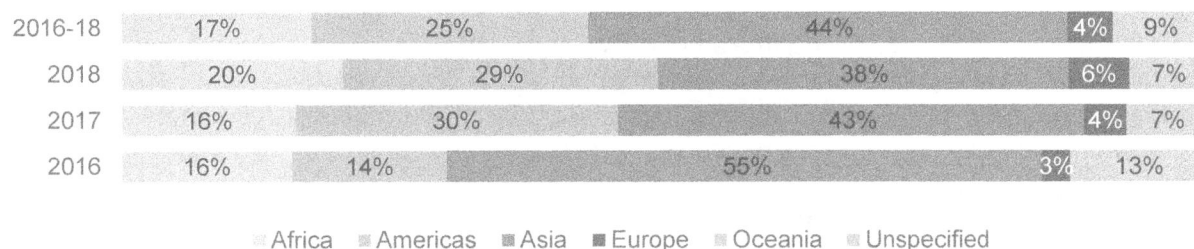

Year	Africa	Americas	Asia	Europe	Oceania	Unspecified
2016-18	17%	25%	44%		4%	9%
2018	20%	29%	38%		6%	7%
2017	16%	30%	43%		4%	7%
2016	16%	14%	55%		3%	13%

Africa Americas Asia Europe Oceania Unspecified

Note: The regions cover only developing countries as defined in Annex C.
Source: OECD Development Assistance Committee statistics as well as complementary reporting to the OECD.

3.6. By income group

Over 2016-18, 90% of country-allocable (i.e. excluding regional activities) private climate finance mobilised by developed countries benefitted MICs, with a strong focus on UMICs (56%) (Figure 3.7). HICs benefitted from 7% of private climate finance mobilised per year on average, LICs only 3%. Moreover, only 5% of total private climate finance mobilised by developed countries during 2016-18 was for the LDCs and 1% for the SIDS (Figure 3.7). These trends are very similar to those observed for private finance mobilised reported as non-climate.

Figure 3.7. Private climate finance mobilised by income group and year (2016-18, %)

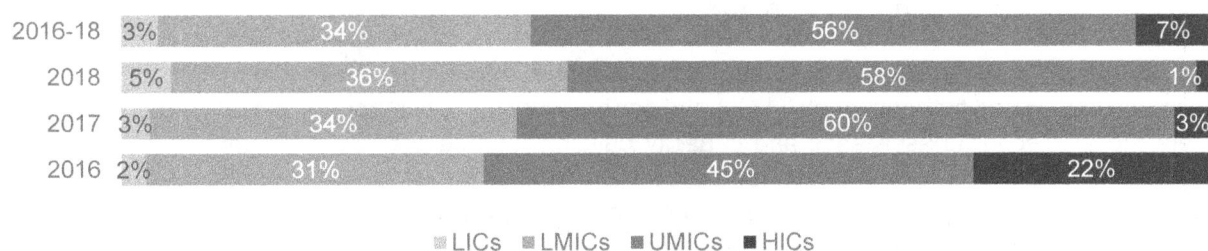

Year	LICs	LMICs	UMICs	HICs
2016-18	3%	34%	56%	7%
2018	5%	36%	58%	1%
2017	3%	34%	60%	3%
2016	2%	31%	45%	22%

LICs LMICs UMICs HICs

Note: Only country-allocable climate finance (79% of the total over 2016-18) is included in this chart.
Source: OECD Development Assistance Committee statistics as well as complementary reporting to the OECD.

Box 3.1. Private philanthropic finance for climate action in developing countries

Private philanthropic foundations constitute an emerging source of finance for climate action in developing countries. Since these organisations are funded from private sources (e.g. donations by high-net-worth individuals and companies, investment returns, royalties, or lottery subscriptions), the climate finance they provide is not accounted for in volumes of public climate finance presented in this report. As the financing activities of such foundations is typically not associated with public climate finance interventions, they are also unlikely to be captured as part of the mobilised private finance component.

The information presented here offers insights on the allocation of climate-related finance from philanthropic foundations headquartered in developed countries, based on new OECD DAC statistics on private philanthropy for development. In 2018, thirty-three of the largest foundations active in developing countries provided USD 0.6 billion of climate-related finance (8% of the foundations development-related commitments, which totalled USD 6.9 billion) (OECD, 2020[17]). The data, available since 2017 and collected based on the Rio marker methodology (OECD, 2016[18]), suggest that in 2017-18 foundations focused more on mitigation (53%) than on adaptation (13%), with a 34% share for cross-cutting activities targeting both objectives.

Figure 3.8. Private philanthropy by climate focus (2017-18, %)

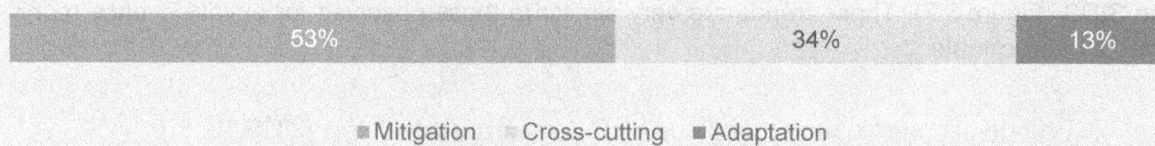

53%	34%	13%

■ Mitigation ■ Cross-cutting ■ Adaptation

Source: OECD Development Assistance Committee statistics.

These funds mainly related to grants supporting projects and programmes implemented by NGOs, research institutes and other channels (46%) and general support to civil society organisations working on climate (46%). Technical assistance and capacity building represented approximately 2% of the yearly average and programme-related investments less than 1%. In terms of sectors, support by foundations to climate action focused primarily on clean energy and sustainable agriculture as well as on broader environmental policy, including climate governance.

Notes

[1] Although the regions identified often group countries and territories sharing certain attributes, they differ significantly in terms of size, population, income, GNI, and other statistical categories. As a result, such regions should only be viewed as a tool that facilitates geographic analyses. See Annex C for further information.

Annex A. Methodological framework

The accounting framework used in this report is consistent with the one used for previous OECD reports. The framework was initially developed in 2015 to estimate climate finance provided and mobilised by developed countries to developing countries in 2013-14 (OECD, 2015[2]). The framework was used subsequently in the 2019 report, which extended the estimated period to 2017 (OECD, 2019[1]). It is also consistent with the outcome of the UNFCCC COP24 as regards the modalities for the accounting of financial resources provided and mobilised through public interventions (UNFCCC, 2019[3]). For a full breakdown of the framework, please refer to (OECD, 2019[1]).

This framework operates with the concepts of 'developed' and 'developing' countries. The latter are defined, for the purpose of this report and previous reports, by combining the UNFCCC non-Annex I list of countries and the OECD DAC list of ODA recipients (OECD, 2015[2]; OECD, 2019[19]). Annex 3 of this report defines both country groupings in detail and lists individual countries and territories pertaining to these categories.

The figures of total climate finance provided and mobilised by developed countries for climate action in developing countries are based on four distinct components (Figure A A.1.):

- Bilateral public climate finance, which consists of public climate finance commitments (beyond export credits) by developed countries for developing countries. Such commitments are made either directly, or through intermediaries (NGOs and civil society, networks, partnerships, universities and research institutes, private for-profit institutions and other bilateral channels) (flow A.1), or as earmarked (non-core) funding through multilateral channels (flow A.2). The data are sourced from developed countries' Biennial Reports (BRs) to the UNFCCC.

- Multilateral public climate finance provided to developing countries that is attributable to developed countries. This component includes climate finance outflows from multilateral development banks (MDBs) and multilateral climate funds (flow B.2) to developing countries, as well as climate-specific contributions by developed countries to multilateral bodies for which climate outflow data are unavailable (flow B.1). Climate finance outflows from MDBs are sourced from activity-level multilateral outflows recorded in the OECD DAC statistics on development finance. Climate-specific contributions by developed countries to multilateral bodies are sourced from developed countries' BRs to the UNFCCC.

- Officially supported climate-related export credits, which consist of trade-related financial support extended by developed countries' export credit agencies for climate-related projects in developing countries (flow C). These data are primarily sourced from activity-level export credit transactions recorded in the OECD Export Credit Group database.

- Private climate finance mobilised attributable to developed countries consists of finance from private sources mobilised by bilateral and multilateral public finance interventions in support of climate activities in developing countries (flow D). These data are primarily sourced from the OECD DAC statistics on development finance, which collects this information at the activity-level.

The OECD DAC and OECD ECG databases are dynamic, which implies that they can accommodate data modifications and updates if needed and requested by the providers. Therefore, the data underpinning this report's figures may have been subject to revisions since their first publication. Nevertheless, this report does not revise figures for the years 2013-17 and does not consider any potential revisions to 2013-2017 data implemented in the databases.

Figure A A.1. Simplified illustration of international development and climate finance architecture

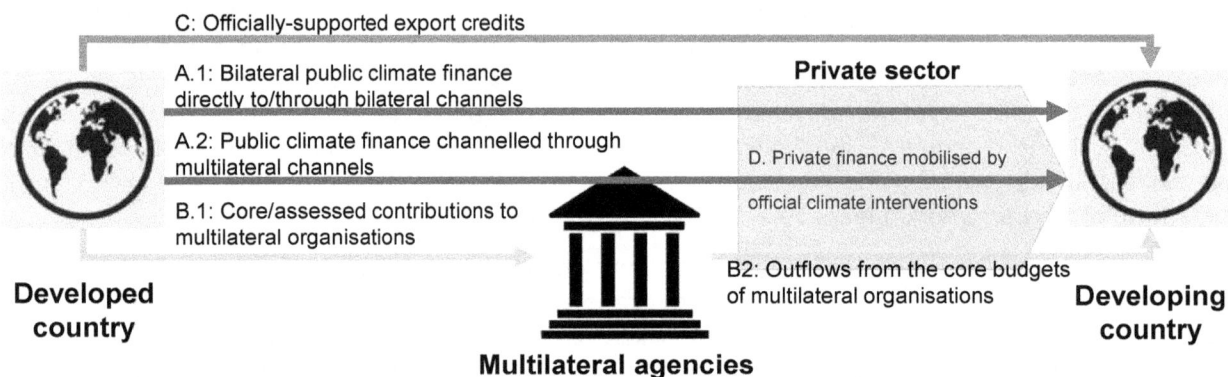

Note: Outflows from the core budget of multilateral organisations and private finance mobilised by multilateral organisations are adjusted to only reflect the share attributable to developed countries.

Annex B. Data sources and methodological considerations

This annex presents the climate finance data sources used and the main methodological issues encountered in the process of compiling, collating, and analysing such data. The annex first addresses methodological aspects for each of the four components outlined in Table A B.1 below and, subsequently, offers some cross-cutting considerations.

Table A B.1. Overview of the categories of finance considered and data sources

Category	Coverage	Instruments	Data source
Bilateral public	Climate finance outflows from donor countries' bilateral development finance agencies and institutions	Grants, loans, equity investments (USA only: developmental guarantees)	Biennial reports to the UNFCCC and complementary data submissions
Multilateral public (attributed to developed countries)	Climate finance outflows from multilateral development banks and climate funds attributable to developed countries	Grants, loans, equity investments	OECD Development Assistance Committee statistics (total multilateral outflows); institutions' annual reports (for calculating attribution shares)
Export credits	Climate-related export credits provided by developed countries' official export credit agencies, mostly for renewable energy	Export credit loans, guarantees, and insurance	OECD Export Credit Group statistics and complementary data submissions
Mobilised private (attributed to developed countries)	Private finance mobilised by bilateral and multilateral public climate finance	Private finance mobilised by grants, loans, equity and developmental guarantees	OECD Development Assistance Committee statistics and complementary data submissions

Note: Bilateral providers include: Australia, Austria, Belgium, Bulgaria, Canada, Cyprus, Czech Republic, Denmark, Estonia, European Union (European Commission and European Development Fund), Finland, France, Germany, Greece, Hungary, Iceland, Ireland, Italy, Japan, Latvia, Lithuania, Luxembourg, Malta, Monaco, Netherlands, New Zealand, Norway, Poland, Portugal, Romania, Slovak Republic, Slovenia, Spain, Sweden, Switzerland, United Kingdom and United States. Multilateral development banks include: African Development Bank (AfDB), African Development Fund (AfDF), Asian Development Bank (ADB), Asian Infrastructure Investment Bank (AIIB), Council of Europe Development Bank (CEB), Development Bank of Latin America (CAF), European Bank for Reconstruction and Development (EBRD), European Investment Bank (EIB), IDB Invest, Inter-American Development Bank (IDB), International Bank for Reconstruction and Development (IBRD), International Development Association (IDA), the International Finance Corporation (IFC), Multilateral Investment Guarantee Agency (MIGA) and Private Infrastructure Development Group (PIDG). Multilateral climate funds include: Adaptation Fund, Climate Investment Funds (CIFs), Green Climate Fund (GCF), Global Environment Facility (GEF) and Nordic Development Fund (NDF). Other multilateral bodies include: the Intergovernmental Panel on Climate Change, the Montreal Protocol, United Nations Programmes, Specialised Agencies and Funds, e.g. International Fund for Agriculture Development, (IFAD), United Nations Framework Convention on Climate Change (UNFCCC) and other. Providers of climate-related export credits include: Austria, Belgium, Canada, Czech Republic, Denmark, Finland, France, Germany, Italy, Japan, Netherlands, Poland, Spain and United States. Mobilised private includes: private finance mobilised by bilateral and multilateral providers listed above.

Bilateral public flows

The bilateral climate finance component includes annual financial commitments (or sometimes disbursements) for 2013-2018 from developed countries to developing countries' governments, NGOs and civil society, research institutes, private sector, networks and public-private partnerships operating in developing countries. Finance listed as "bilateral climate finance" excludes all forms of export credit financing to avoid any double counting with the separate export credit component. It also excludes any coal-related financing. With the exception of the United States, bilateral climate finance data also exclude developmental guarantees, which are accounted separately for their mobilisation effect under the mobilised private finance component.

Data sources and geographical coverage

2018 bilateral climate finance data are in principle sourced from Table 7(b) of the Common Tabular Format (CTF) tables[1] that Annex I Parties have submitted to the UNFCCC to accompany their Fourth Biennial Report (BR) to the UNFCCC. According to the UNFCCC guidelines for the preparation of BRs, only Annex II Parties[2] are required to biennially report information on annual levels of financial support provided using a CTF (UNFCCC, 2012[20]). The bilateral climate finance component in this report includes 2013-2018 financial flows, as reported by Annex II Parties and by a number of other Annex I Parties.[3] The Fourth BRs and the accompanying CTFs were submitted to the UNFCCC in 2020 and include, *inter alia,* climate finance data for the biennium 2017-2018. As of September 2020, all Annex II Parties except for Iceland and the United States have submitted a Fourth BR and its accompanying CTFs to the UNFCCC. Therefore, bilateral climate finance from the United States and Iceland for 2018 was estimated as the average of the respective 2016/2017 contributions. Bilateral climate finance data for 2013-2017 reflect figures presented in (OECD, 2019[1]) and (OECD, 2015[2]), and have not been updated or revised for the purpose of this report. In particular, data for 2014 and 2017 were sourced from countries in advance of their official reporting to the UNFCCC based on bilateral exchanges between the OECD and donor Parties. Post-checks, however, demonstrated only marginal variations with the final data reported to the UNFCCC.

Through Table 7(b) of the CTFs, countries report information on the provision of public financial support through bilateral, regional, and other channels. When reporting information on bilateral climate finance flows using table 7(b) of the CTF, countries are to provide information on (i) Recipient country/region/project/programme, (ii) Climate-specific amount, (iii) Status, (iv) Funding source, (v) Financial instrument, (vi) Type of support and (vii) Sector. The set of CTFs submitted by each country is made publicly available on the UNFCCC website as MS Excel files (.xlsx). The BRs and the documentation boxes that accompany the CTFs allow countries to report further information on methodologies and definitions adopted by countries to estimate financial flows, notably to explain how they define funds as climate-specific.

Methodological considerations

While Annex II countries are required to report bilateral climate finance flows to the UNFCCC using a common format (that is, Table 7(b) of the CTFs), working in-depth with the data reported as done for the present report makes it possible to identify significant inconsistencies in terms of methodologies, categorisations, and definitions adopted across countries. This is because UNFCCC reporting guidelines provide some leeway in terms of climate finance reporting. Most OECD DAC members base their reporting to the UNFCCC on the climate-related development finance data they report to the OECD DAC. Yet, bilateral climate finance data reported to the UNFCCC are neither as detailed (fewer data fields) nor as standardised as data reported to the OECD DAC statistical system.

It is observed that climate finance reporting to the UNFCCC varies across countries in three main areas that have a significant impact on the amount reported:

- **Currency conversion**: The figures presented in this report are based on reporting by countries in USD, when available. Exchange rates used to estimate amounts in USD vary across countries. Most countries use the "Annual Average Dollar Exchange Rates for DAC Members" for reporting their climate finance data in USD. Where that was not the case, the relative difference between amounts in USD, as reported by countries and conversion based on the "Annual Average Dollar

Exchange Rates for DAC Members," showed only minor variance. Where countries provided climate finance in another currency (Table 7(b) of the CTFs allows countries to report bilateral climate finance in USD and/or in the national currency), the amount was converted using the "Annual Average Dollar Exchange Rates for DAC Members" (Figure A B.1).

- **Commitment and disbursement**: Countries may report either financial commitments or disbursements to the UNFCC. Most choose to report either on "disbursed" or on "committed" climate finance. However, a limited number of countries combine both, depending on the financial instrument. As a result, figures of bilateral climate finance presented in this report are based on a combination of commitment and disbursement data. Exchange of information with countries and ad-hoc requests for further clarification has ensured that double counting has been avoided for countries that reported both. Overall, disbursement data almost exclusively relate to grants.

- **Climate-specific amounts:** Table 7(b) of the CTFs requires countries to report information on the climate-specific amount of a contribution; that is the share of a contribution that targets climate change specifically. To calculate the climate-specific component of a contribution, most countries apply a coefficient to scale down the total value of a project, for which climate change is not the only objective. Countries adopt different approaches to calculate the climate-specific amount of a contribution. A limited number of countries currently undertake ad-hoc assessments for each project, whereas a number of countries use a range of fixed coefficients (e.g., 30%, 40%, 100%) that apply by default depending on whether climate change was the only, primary, or secondary objective pursued by the project. In order to enhance transparency on climate-related development finance reported to the UNFCCC by DAC members, the OECD DAC conducted a voluntary survey in 2018 and 2020. Based on responses received by 19 out of 30 DAC members, the results of the 2020 survey (forthcoming) show that in most cases, countries apply fixed coefficients to any activity marked principal or significant with the Rio markers on climate change.

Data harmonisation and quality checks

The UNFCCC guidelines for the reporting of financial information by Parties included in Annex I to the Convention (decision 9/CP.21) (UNFCCC, 2015[21]), and the guiding footnotes to table 7(b) of the CTFs provide limited guidance to countries on how to fill in the CTFs. Each reporting parameter of table 7(b) includes a list of standardised categorisations (labels) that Annex I countries can use to report on different aspects of a contribution.

However, data labels and descriptions used vary significantly across countries, particularly for recipients and sectors. For the purpose of this report, and to allow for meaningful aggregation and analysis of data, bilateral climate finance data included by Annex I countries in the relevant CTFs had to be harmonised and re-coded into a set of defined categorisations. These encompass:

- **Status:** Decision 9/CP.21 aligned the labels of the reporting parameter "status" of support to other existing international methodologies (UNFCCC, 2015[21]). Accordingly, since 2015, countries are to report contributions as "committed" and "disbursed". No variance across countries was observed in the use of labels, and no additional harmonisation work was needed.

- **Funding source:** Labels made available by table 7(b) include: ODA, OOF, Other. Limited variance in the use of these labels was observed across countries. When countries report a contribution as a combination of ODA and OOF, or as "other", exchange of information took place with donor countries to clarify the source.

- **Financial instrument:** Financial instrument labels made available by table 7(b) were: grant, concessional loan, non-concessional loan, equity, and other. A number of countries used sub-variants of these categorisations, e.g. "syndicated loan", "interest subsidy", etc. Financial instruments have been re-coded according to the categorisation of loans, grants, equity, export credits, and development guarantees.[4] When countries reported the financial instrument of a contribution as "other", exchange of information took place with donor countries to clarify the financial instrument.

- **Type of finance:** Type of finance categorisations made available by table 7(b) include: mitigation, adaptation, cross-cutting. No variance across countries was observed in the labels used, and no additional harmonisation work was needed.

- **Sectors:** Type of sectoral categorisations made available by table 7(b) include: energy, transport, industry, agriculture, forestry, water and sanitation, cross-cutting, other. To facilitate comparability with other climate finance components included in this report, sectors were re-coded to the highest level of granularity available so as to correspond to standardised DAC sectoral classification. Great variation in the use of sectoral labels was observed. Some countries report sectors using the DAC purpose codes alone (e.g. "232"), other countries report jointly the DAC purpose code and the sectoral category (e.g. "232 – Energy generation, renewable sources"), and other countries report using the sectoral labels that are prompted by the CTFs (e.g. "Energy). For 2018 data alone, countries used 281 different sectoral definitions, which were subsequently re-coded into 83 DAC sectors.

- **Recipients:** The CTF reporting field "recipient country/region/project/programme" does not include any standardised labels for countries to use. Because of the broad reporting scope of this reporting parameter, great variance is observed across countries in terms of reporting format, level of detail and wording. Furthermore, different countries use different spellings or languages to indicate the same recipient country. For example, at least 19 different spellings were observed to indicate the Democratic Republic of the Congo. As a result, the harmonisation of recipients for 2018 data alone implied the re-coding of virtually all recipients based on a combination of keyword searches and, where needed, manual re-coding. Recipient countries were re-coded as regions or sub-regions when multiple countries belonging to the same geographical area were listed for a single contribution.

For a number of observations, it was not possible to harmonise and re-code sectors and recipients. The recipient country and/or sector of these contributions were marked as "Unspecified" under either category. This was the case for a number of contributions, for which activity-level data were not available. For example, a number of contributions were marked as being directed to a list of (specified) multiple countries belonging to different geographical areas and/or sectors. In such cases, and as it was not specified by countries, it was not possible to assess what shares of the contribution would target each recipient/sector.

To ensure data quality, consistency and comparability, information exchanges took place throughout the process between the OECD and individual donor countries, e.g., to identify and exclude coal-related financing, or to identify and exclude delegated grants from the GCF to avoid double counting with the multilateral outflow component. One country has included in its table 7(b) figures for climate finance mobilised. These were excluded to avoid double counting with the mobilised climate finance component.

Finally, a number of countries include earmarked (i.e., multi-bilateral) contributions to UN agencies, NGOs, and IGOs in table 7(b) of the CTF. As there are no commonly-agreed UNFCCC guidelines on where to report on multi-bilateral contributions in the CTFs, where these contributions were reported in table 7(b), they have been included in the bilateral climate finance figures. For these contributions, the recipients were marked as "global/unallocated".

Potential for facilitating and improving data analysis

While standardised reporting across countries of status and type of finance, financial instruments and funding source has significantly improved over time, a number of challenges related to the reporting of recipients and sectors continue hindering data analysis. To enhance the transparency of reporting and to facilitate data analysis, as well as to limit the risk of errors, it would be helpful if countries were to report information on bilateral climate finance in a format that could be easily read and processed by a computer ("machine-readable"), limiting the need for manual work in the context of data harmonisation. For this purpose, as analysed in more depth by the OECD/IEA Climate Change Expert Group (Falduto and Ellis, 2019[22]), it would be useful to ensure that:

- Data are reported, to the extent possible, according to standardised labels prompted by the CTFs.
- Recipient countries and/or regions are indicated in a dedicated data field, separately from the project and programme title. Given that this reporting option is not possible within current CTFs, including the name of a country at the beginning of a text string (e.g. in the "Recipient country/region/project/programme" field) would facilitate the identification and isolation of the recipient for data analysis purposes.
- Data are reported, wherever applicable, at the activity-level. This implies avoiding reporting contributions aggregated per, e.g., disbursing agency.

Multilateral public climate finance

The multilateral public climate component covers climate-related commitments by multilateral development banks (MDBs), multilateral climate funds, as well as other multilateral organisations, sourced from their core resources (sometimes referred to as ordinary capital), and subsequently attributed to developed countries. Outflows from trust funds and special-purpose programmes administered by multilateral organisations are not included in the multilateral public component. Inflows to such funds and programmes are considered as provider countries' bilateral climate finance and are, in principle, reported in Table 7(b) of the CTF tables submitted to the UNFCCC. Where applicable, such inflows to special-purpose funds and programmes are presented under the "bilateral public" finance component. There are currently no exhaustive and internationally standardised project-level data available on the outflows (including climate-related) from trust funds and similar vehicles managed by multilateral organisations. This situation is likely to improve in the coming years with new international statistical efforts, such as the new measure Total Official Support for Sustainable Development (TOSSD) (OECD TOSSD, 2020[23]). In addition, the figures also include contributions by developed countries (inflows) to multilateral organisations, for which standardised climate finance outflow data are unavailable at present; this is particularly the case for specialised UN agencies, such as UNDP or UN Environment.

The multilateral public climate component includes all modalities and financial instruments that constitute long-term financial flows. This includes grants, equity investments, mezzanine/hybrid finance and debt instrument with a maturity of over one year. Short-term debt operations (notably short-term trade finance operations) are excluded. To avoid double counting across individual finance components, multilateral guarantees and other unfunded contingent liabilities are presented under the component on private finance mobilised in case they cover private finance. They are excluded in case they cover public finance.

Data sources and geographical coverage

Data on multilateral core budget outflows are sourced from the standardised activity-level data on development finance collected by the OECD DAC. The geographic coverage of the multilateral outflow data is limited to countries and territories included on the DAC List of ODA Recipients (OECD, 2020[14]). As illustrated in Annex 3, the DAC List of ODA Recipients significantly overlaps but is not identical to the list of non-Annex I Parties to the UNFCCC. However, a comparison of the OECD DAC data coverage with data available on other platforms, such as the International Aid Transparency Initiative (IATI), revealed that only negligible amounts of climate finance are left out due to the geographic inconsistency of the DAC and non-Annex I lists. Moreover, concerning multilateral agencies for which no project-level outflow data are available, the analysis uses inflows included by Annex I Parties in table 7(a) of the Biennial Reports to the UNFCCC.

Multilateral outflows reported to OECD DAC statistics include a range of statistical categories beyond climate change mitigation and adaptation. These include standardised information on, for instance, recipients, sectors, instruments, and channels of delivery and modalities (e.g. projects versus technical assistance). Such standardised data were extensively used in this report to conduct disaggregated analyses. On the other hand, the only information available for core contributions to multilateral organisations reported according to the BR's reporting guidelines in table 7(a) of the CTFs was the climate focus.

Methodological considerations

Reporting to the OECD DAC on multilateral outflows is based on statistical data fields and underlying definitional standards. This results in a dataset that is more coherent than for bilateral climate finance reported to the UNFCCC, notably in terms of point of measurement (all commitment based), currency conversion and sectoral classifications. However, in terms of tracking climate finance, multilateral organisations currently report to the OECD DAC statistical system based on two different methods:

- The Rio markers methodology, which is designed to identify activities that mainstream the objectives of the UNFCCC into development co-operation (OECD DAC, 2016[10]). Used initially by DAC members only, most multilateral climate funds (e.g. Adaptation Fund, GCF, GEF, NDF) based their climate-related reporting for the years covered by this report on the DAC Rio markers method. This approach accounts for the full face value of activities assessed as having climate change mitigation and/or adaptation as their principal (primary) or significant (secondary) objective, as opposed to activities assessed as not targeting the UNFCCC objectives and unscreened activities.

- The MDB methodologies for tracking climate change adaptation and mitigation finance (MDBs, 2020[4]). While these two MDB approaches fundamentally differ in nature, they are intended to deliver quantified indications of the extent to which individual activities contribute to or promote adaptation and/or mitigation (multilateral climate components). The MDB method on adaptation does so by capturing the incremental cost of adaptation activities. The MDB method for tracking mitigation finance is based on a "positive" list of activities in sectors that reduce greenhouse gas (GHG) emissions and are compatible with low-emission development.

A key methodological point behind the multilateral public climate finance figures is considering only the share of multilateral climate commitments attributable to developed countries. Multilateral institutions are typically funded or capitalised by core contributions from both developed and developing countries. Institutions that operate with a financial business model use these contributions as a basis for raising finance from the capital markets. A specific methodology is, therefore, needed to calculate, for each institution, the share of its outflows attributable to developed countries, with the remainder being attributable to developing countries. Such calculation takes into account the concessional and non-concessional nature of multilateral finance, most recent and cumulative replenishment participations by individual countries, as well as, where applicable, the organisations' capacity to raise funds from the capital markets (TWG, 2015[24]). The resulting attribution shares can be found in Table A B.2. These attribution percentages are also applied to the amounts mobilised from the private sector by the multilateral agencies' interventions.[5]

Table A B.2. Calculated share of multilateral climate finance attributable to developed countries

Type of institution	Institution name	Abbreviation	2015	2018
Multilateral Development Banks	African Development Bank	AfDB	59.0%	58.2%
	African Development Fund	AfDF	94%	93.6%
	Asian Development Bank	AsDB	71.0%	71.4%
	Asian Development Bank Special Fund	AsDF	96.0%	95.2%
	Asian Infrastructure Investment Bank	AIIB	N/A	27.3%
	Council of Europe Development Bank	CEB	N/A	98.4%
	Development Bank of Latin America	CAF	N/A	5.1%
	European Bank for Reconstruction and Development	EBRD	89.0%	88.8%
	European Investment Bank	EIB	99.0%	98.6%
	International Bank for Reconstruction and Development	IBRD	70.0%	67.9%
	International Development Association	IDA	95.0%	92.8%
	Inter-American Development Bank	IADB	74.0%	73.6%
	Inter-American Development Bank Special Fund		73.0%	72.5%
	IDB Invest		N/A	33.6%
	International Finance Corporation	IFC	64.1%	64.1%
	Multilateral Investment Guarantee Agency	MIGA	64.3%	64.2%
	Private Infrastructure Development Group	PIDG	N/A	100.0%
Multilateral Climate Fund	Adaptation Fund	AF	100.0%	100.0%
	Climate Investment Funds	CIFs	100.0%	99.0%
	Global Environment Facility Trust Funds	GEF	98.0%	98.0%
	Global Environment Facility Least Developed Countries Fund		100.0%	99.9%
	Global Environment Facility Special Climate Change Fund		100.0%	99.5%
	Green Climate Fund (GCF)	GCF	N/A	99.6%
	International Fund for Agricultural Development (IFAD)	IFAD	N/A	74.2%
	Nordic Development Fund (NDF)	NDF	100.0%	100.0%

Notes: The 2015 percentages apply to 2013, 2014 and 2015 multilateral climate finance outflow data. The 2018 percentages apply to 2016, 2017 and 2018 data. The merger of the AsDB ordinary capital resources (OCR) balance sheet with the lending operations of the AsDF became effective at the start of 2017. Climate finance outflows for the GCF, the IDB Invest (previously Inter-American Investment Corporation; IIC) and the AIIB were first recorded in OECD DAC statistics in 2015, 2016 and 2017 respectively. Climate finance outflows from IFAD, CEB and CAF were first included in the present figures in 2018 (figures for previous years include developed countries' inflows to IFAD and did not cover CAF and CEB altogether).
Source: OECD calculations based on annual reports and websites of each of the listed institutions; see also (OECD, 2019[19]) and (TWG, 2015[24]).

Potential for facilitating and improving data analysis

In principle, data reported by multilateral organisations to the OECD DAC, including on climate, are collected and made publicly available at the activity-level. However, the IFC raised confidentiality concerns regarding its 2018 climate commitment data. Tailor-made legal and technical solutions were required to overcome these constraints, enabling the IFC to share these data with the OECD. Information on some projects were, nevertheless, provided as aggregates due to their strictly confidential nature. These aggregates accounted for 15% of the total IFC climate commitments in 2018. Similarly, IDB Invest has been providing anonymised activity-level data on its outflow commitments and the multilateral climate components. Discussions with IFC and IDB Invest were on-going at the time of writing of this report, to explore ways to lift some of these restrictions, which prevent the OECD from conducting basic data quality assurance work.

More generally, further transparency on MDB climate finance data would benefit the international community. While MDBs report their outflows to the OECD based on DAC statistical standards, they have also since 2013 published their climate finance numbers in dedicated annual joint MDB reports (MDBs, 2020[4]). For most of the MDBs, the accounting basis used to develop the joint MDB reports is different from that of the OECD DAC, e.g. in terms of point of measurement, geographical scope, or instrument coverage. The joint MDB reports are intended to communicate on MDBs' performance to the shareholders, rather than provide international statistics relevant to UNFCCC discussions. Accordingly, MDBs currently do not make their activity-level datasets that underpin the joint MDB reports publicly available, which makes it challenging to conduct comparisons and partial reconciliation with the data recorded in the OECD DAC database. Overall, sharing transparent and granular data to the OECD is critical for harmonisation and comparability purposes.

Officially-supported export credits

Officially-supported export credits are the third component included in the report. Although extended primarily to support national export and facilitate international trade, export credits can also contribute to climate action by supporting transactions for climate-related sectors and projects with climate mitigation or adaptation benefits. Data on climate-related export credits originate from two sources:

- The vast majority of the data are sourced from the OECD Export Credit Group's (ECG) database on officially-supported export credits, which contains activity-level transaction data reported by official export credit agencies (ECAs). The ECG statistics includes two main types of export credit transactions: loans extended directly by ECAs and loan guaranteed (or insurances) by ECAs. Both types are accounted for on their face value and on a gross basis. Importantly, the ECG database only covers export credits with a repayment term of two years or more that were provided in conformity with the Arrangement on Officially Supported Export Credits (OECD, 2020[25]). For the purpose of this report, only export credit data reported as explicitly targeting renewable energy, climate change mitigation and adaptation, and water projects were included. In practice, such data covers almost only renewable energy-related transactions.

- Some countries provide export support outside of that reported under the aforementioned Arrangement, i.e. beyond the ECG database. Six countries reported such complementary data: Canada, Italy, Japan, Spain, Switzerland and the United States. These countries either provided one-off data inputs either directly to the OECD for the purpose of this report or by including export credits in their biennial climate finance reporting to the UNFCCC. The reported data mainly related to renewable energy, with only a few transactions in the water and sanitation, and transport sectors. Where relevant, export credit transactions supporting coal-related activities were excluded.

To avoid double counting across these data sources, all export credit data that were made available to the authors of this report were carefully reviewed, cross-checked and netted out. For example, export-credit activities reported by countries to the UNFCCC were excluded from the bilateral climate finance component and included in the export credit one if not already captured by the OECD export credit database. In terms of general methodological considerations, export credit data are collected on a commitment basis. Furthermore, data sourced from the ECG database are converted to USD using monthly average exchange rates relating to the monthly commitment.

Private finance mobilised by official climate finance interventions

Data source and coverage

Under a high-level mandate from ministers, the OECD DAC has developed an international standard for measuring the amounts mobilised from the private sector by official development finance interventions, including for climate. Work has been carried out jointly with the OECD-led Research Collaborative on Tracking Finance for Climate Action, as well as in close collaboration with experts from bilateral development finance institutions, aid agencies and ministries, as well as the MDBs and other multilateral organisations. Based on multiple years and successive rounds of research, stakeholder consultations, surveys, methodological developments, and implementation, the methodology is considered comprehensive and, since 2017, has been fully implemented in the regular CRS data collection. The Working Party on Development Finance Statistics (WP-STAT) will continue to fine-tune the methodology where needed (e.g. on how to account for the role of technical assistance in mobilisation schemes).

The scope of the OECD DAC methodology for measuring the amounts mobilised from the private sector covers the main mechanisms used by development finance providers, including syndicated loans, guarantees, credit lines, direct investment in companies or special purpose vehicles (SPVs), shares in collective investment vehicles (CIVs) and simple co-financing arrangements. In order to avoid double-counting at the international level when multiple official financiers invest in the same project or vehicle together with the private sector, the amounts mobilised from the private sector are attributed following an instrument-specific approach in order to take into account the role (e.g. arranger of syndications) and position (investment seniority) played by each official actor. In addition, as a matter of principle, the mobilisation methods take into account the role played by all official actors involved, including both international and domestic public agencies (e.g. national development banks).

Consistently with data coverage that underpinned previous OECD figures of private climate finance mobilised in 2016 and 2017 (OECD, 2019[1]), almost all DAC members and multilateral agencies that work with the private sector report their mobilisation data to OECD DAC. The core reporting fields in this context include (1) the mechanism used, (2) the origin of funds mobilised and (3) the amounts mobilised from the private sector. These statistical collections do not include the identity of private financiers mobilised nor the terms and conditions of the finance they extended. In principle, these data are shared as part of annual data reporting by these providers in the context of the more general methodological framework agreed by the DAC Working Party on Development Finance Statistics (WP-STAT).

Table A B.3. Mechanisms and instruments in the OECD DAC measure or private finance mobilised

Mechanism	Typical financial instruments used by official finance providers	Typical financial instruments used by private financiers
Syndicated loans	Standard loans, subordinated loans	Standard loans, subordinated loans
Guarantees	Guarantees and other unfunded contingent liabilities	Common equity, shares in CIVs, mezzanine finance, standards loans, bonds and other debt instruments
Credit lines	Standard loans, subordinated loans	Standard loans, subordinated loans to the local finance institution; equity of the end-borrowers
Shares in CIVs	Shares in CIVs, debt instruments and mezzanine finance (rarely)	Shares in CIVs, debt instrument and mezzanine finance (rarely)
Direct investment in companies	Common equity, mezzanine finance, standard loans, bonds and other debt instruments	Common equity, mezzanine finance, standard loans, bonds and other debt instruments
Simple co-financing arrangements	Standard grants, standard loans	Standard grants, standard loans
Project finance	Common equity, mezzanine finance, standard loans and other debt instruments, guarantees	Common equity, mezzanine finance, standard loans and other debt instruments

Source: OECD Development Assistance Committee statistics as well as complementary reporting to the OECD.

Two countries (Italy and Japan) have provided data on their private mobilisation for specific years on an ad-hoc basis. Switzerland also included some mobilisation figures in its Fourth Biennial Reports to the UNFCCC. Moreover:

- IFC could only share its private mobilisation data for 2017 through a physical data secure room due to confidentiality constraints. The context and limitations of this data sharing modality are thoroughly described in the previous edition of this report (OECD, 2019[1]). Breakdowns were obtained by year, financing mechanism, climate focus, and main region group (i.e. Asia, Africa, Americas, Europe and Oceania). Data on sectoral distribution were not retrieved. For 2018, IFC submitted its mobilisation data to the OECD under a data-sharing agreement.

- IDB Invest and AIIB could not share data on private finance mobilised for 2018 due to confidentiality and/or internal capacity reasons. At the time of writing this report, discussions were on-going with IDB Invest on a data-sharing agreement for their future reporting on mobilisation. To fill in this statistical gap, the private climate finance mobilised by IDB Invest and AIIB was estimated by the authors using publicly available sources, including the institutions' annual reports and individual project documentation available in the public domain.

Methodological considerations

Data on private climate mobilisation collected by the DAC or estimated for the purpose of this report are converted to USD using the nominal annual average exchange rates. These are presented in Table A C.4.

The point of measurement for private finance mobilisation is, in general, at the time when the information becomes available to all co-financiers in individual projects (e.g. commitments or financial closure). While the financing structure of syndicated loans is typically known at the commitment stage, the mobilisation effect of shares in CIVs and direct investment in companies can stretch over a certain period of time, which sometimes requires reporting on a disbursement or ex-post basis.

Similarly to the multilateral public finance, private climate finance mobilised by multilateral providers only reflects the shares attributed to developed countries (see Table A B.2). The climate relevance of mobilised private finance is reported by providers to the OECD DAC based on either the DAC Rio marker or the MDB methodologies. The extent to which private finance mobilised contributes to climate change mitigation and/or adaptation is determined by the climate relevance or percentage of the official finance intervention mobilising private finance. For example, if an MDB loan with a mitigation component of 75% mobilises private finance, this same percentage is applied to the private amount mobilised. Amounts of private finance mobilised tagged for climate based on Rio markers are accounted for at their face value.

Potential for facilitating and improving data analysis

DAC members and the multilateral community have been sharing data on their private mobilisation with the OECD at the project level since the inception of this work in 2015, following the OECD DAC statistical standards and definitions for comparability purposes. These data were primarily used for various analytical outputs of the OECD, presenting highly aggregated trends. To respond to increasing needs for transparency in the development and climate finance communities, in 2018, DAC members agreed on data disclosure rules that allow for using those data by a broader range of stakeholders.

In recent years, however, some MDBs indicated that they face data confidentiality constraints when reporting to the OECD on amounts mobilised from the private sector, including for climate action. A working group involving MDBs, DAC members, and the OECD Secretariat was launched in 2019 to address these issues and explore solutions for the MDBs to continue providing these data to the OECD. The objective of the group is to agree on data disclosure rules for the MDBs' mobilisation data while preserving the integrity of the OECD DAC statistical system and meeting information needs by countries, the private sector, and the civil society. Pending the agreement and implementation of such solutions, interim individual data sharing and non-disclosure agreements had to be signed with some MDBs for the 2018 data collection on mobilisation, namely the AsDB, EBRD, EIB and IFC.

Exchange rate fluctuations

There were significant exchange rate fluctuations over 2013-18, with a consequent effect on the total climate finance figures. This is particularly relevant for the conversion of the Euro, Japanese Yen, and the Pound Sterling, which are used by the largest climate finance providers. Over 2013-18, these three currencies showed exchange rate fluctuations of over 20% each, taking 2013 as a basis year (Figure A B.1).

Figure A B.1. Exchange rate over 2013-18 per annum vis-à-vis the United States dollar

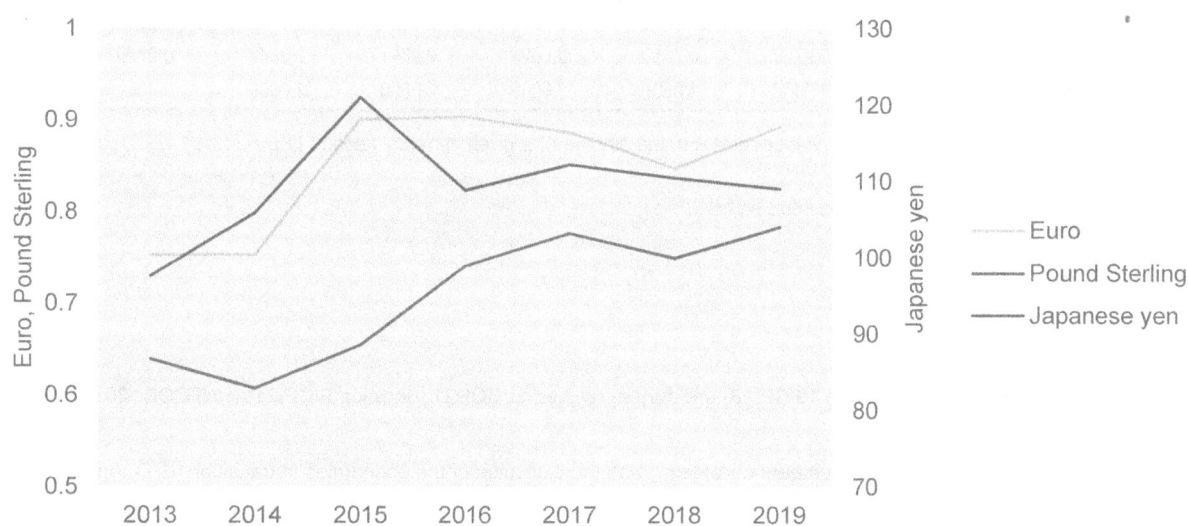

Source: (OECD, 2018[26]).

For further reference, Table A C.4 presents the annual conversion rates *vis-à-vis* the United States dollar used in the context of the DAC statistics and the present report.

Table A B.4. Relevant exchange rates *vis-à-vis* the United States dollar for 2013 to 2018

Currency	2013	2014	2015	2016	2017	2018	2019
Australian dollar	1.0367	1.1094	1.3309	1.3453	1.3049	1.3387	1.4387
Canadian dollar	1.0302	1.1047	1.2783	1.3254	1.2981	1.2961	1.3270
Czech koruna	19.5585	20.7578	24.5926	24.4406	23.3855	21.7298	22.9311
Danish krone	5.6169	5.6187	6.7254	6.7308	6.6018	6.3135	6.6692
Euro	0.7532	0.7537	0.9015	0.9043	0.8871	0.8473	0.8933
Hungarian forint	223.5404	232.6191	279.1926	281.5210	274.4764	270.2212	290.6026
Iceland króna	122.1541	116.6880	131.8961	120.8136	106.8234	108.2693	122.6365
Japanese yen	97.5910	105.8475	121.0023	108.8027	112.1831	110.4378	109.0459
New Zealand dollar	1.2203	1.2058	1.4342	1.4365	1.4074	1.4456	1.5180
Norwegian krone	5.8780	6.3019	8.0643	8.4002	8.2710	8.1348	8.7986
Polish złoty	3.1596	3.1543	3.7702	3.9441	3.7793	3.6114	3.8375
Pound Sterling	0.6396	0.6074	0.6545	0.7410	0.7766	0.7497	0.7836
Swedish krona	6.5132	6.8599	8.4293	8.5565	8.5470	8.6904	9.4559
Swiss franc	0.9268	0.9150	0.9623	0.9851	0.9847	0.9779	0.9938
United States dollar	1.0000	1.0000	1.0000	1.0000	1.0000	1.0000	1.0000

Note: These are nominal annual average exchange rates, i.e. the amount of a given currency needed to purchase 1 USD, calculated as an average of daily rates during a given calendar year.
Source: https://data.oecd.org/conversion/exchange-rates.htm.

Notes

[1] These were agreed at COP18 (decision 19/CP.18) and further revised at COP21 (decision 9/CP.21) (UNFCCC, 2012; UNFCCC, 2015).

[2] Annex II Parties consist of the OECD members of Annex I, with the exclusion of the economies in transition (EIT). Annex II Parties are listed in the 1992 United Nations Framework Convention on Climate Change, amended by decision 26/CP.7: Australia, Austria, Belgium, Canada, Denmark, European Union, Finland, France, Germany, Greece, Iceland, Ireland, Italy, Japan, Luxembourg, Netherlands, New Zealand, Norway, Portugal, Spain, Sweden, Switzerland, United Kingdom, United States.

[3] Czech Republic, Estonia, Hungary, Latvia, Lithuania, Malta, Monaco, Poland, Romania, Slovak Republic and Slovenia.

[4] One country has reported, for a number of concessional loans, the grant equivalent value of the contribution and the remaining part of the loan. For the purpose of this report, the instrument "grant equivalent" has been re-coded as "loan", as figures are based on gross flows, i.e. the face value, of climate finance.

[5] The attribution share for the Multilateral Investment Guarantee Agency (MIGA) is only applied on the amounts mobilised from the private sector by this organisation, as guarantees are not accounted for in the multilateral public climate finance component. Similarly, the attribution share for the Private Infrastructure Development Group (PIDG) is only used in the context of the private climate finance mobilised, since PIDG has been reporting to the OECD DAC on the amounts mobilised from the private sector only.

Annex C. Country groupings

For the purpose of this report's analysis and figures, the following classifications are used:

- "Developed countries", which include Annex II Parties to the Convention, the Member States of the European Union, Lichtenstein and Monaco (Table A C.1)
- "Developing countries", which refer to countries and territories included on the DAC List of ODA Recipients for 2018 development finance (OECD, 2020[14]) and/or on the non-Annex I list of Parties to the UNFCCC (Table A C.2, Table A C.3, and Table A C.4).

Countries and territories that do not fall in these categories (most notably the Russian Federation (Russia) are not covered by the analysis.

Table A C.1. Developed countries

Australia	European Union	Latvia	Portugal
Austria	Finland	Liechtenstein	Romania
Belgium	France	Lithuania	Slovak Republic
Bulgaria	Germany	Luxembourg	Slovenia
Canada	Greece	Malta	Spain
Croatia	Hungary	Monaco	Sweden
Cyprus[12]	Iceland	Netherlands	Switzerland
Czech Republic	Ireland	New Zealand	United Kingdom
Denmark	Italy	Norway	United States
Estonia	Japan	Poland	

Table A C.2. Developing countries: Non-Annex Parties on the DAC List of ODA Recipients

Afghanistan	Dominica	Liberia	Saint Kitts and Nevis
Albania	Dominican Republic	Libya	Saint Lucia
Algeria	Ecuador	Madagascar	Saint Vincent and the Grenadines
Angola	Egypt	Malawi	Samoa
Antigua and Barbuda	El Salvador	Malaysia	Sao Tome and Principe
Argentina	Equatorial Guinea	Maldives	Senegal
Armenia	Eritrea	Mali	Serbia
Azerbaijan	Eswatini	Marshall Islands	Sierra Leone
Bangladesh	Ethiopia	Mauritania	Solomon Islands
Belize	Fiji	Mauritius	Somalia
Benin	Gabon	Mexico	South Africa
Bhutan	Gambia	Micronesia	South Sudan
Bolivia	Georgia	Moldova	Sri Lanka
Bosnia and Herzegovina	Ghana	Mongolia	Sudan
Botswana	Grenada	Montenegro	Suriname
Brazil	Guatemala	Morocco	Syrian Arab Republic
Burkina Faso	Guinea	Mozambique	Tajikistan
Burundi	Guinea-Bissau	Myanmar	Tanzania
Cabo Verde	Guyana	Namibia	Thailand
Cambodia	Haiti	Nauru	Timor-Leste
Cameroon	Honduras	Nepal	Togo
Central African Republic	India	Nicaragua	Tonga
Chad	Indonesia	Niger	Tunisia
China (People's Republic of)	Iran	Nigeria	Turkmenistan
Colombia	Iraq	Niue	Tuvalu
Comoros	Jamaica	North Macedonia	Uganda
Congo	Jordan	Pakistan	Uzbekistan
Cook Islands	Kazakhstan	Palau	Vanuatu
Costa Rica	Kenya	Panama	Venezuela
Côte d'Ivoire	Kiribati	Papua New Guinea	Viet Nam
Cuba	Kyrgyzstan	Paraguay	West Bank and Gaza Strip
Korea	Lao People's Democratic Republic	Peru	Yemen
Democratic Republic of the Congo	Lebanon	Philippines	Zambia
Djibouti	Lesotho	Rwanda	Zimbabwe

Table A C.3. Developing countries: Non-Annex I Parties beyond ODA Recipients

Andorra	Chile	Korea	Trinidad and Tobago
Bahamas	Israel	San Marino	United Arab Emirates
Bahrain	Kuwait	Saudi Arabia	Uruguay
Barbados	Oman	Seychelles	
Brunei Darussalam	Qatar	Singapore	

Table A C.4. Developing countries: ODA Recipients beyond the Non-Annex I Parties

Belarus	Montserrat	Tokelau	Ukraine
Kosovo	Saint Helena	Turkey	Wallis and Futuna

Regions and sub-regions

Section 2 analyses climate finance by region and sub-region. The classifications used in this report are inspired by the M49 standard of the United Nations (UNSD, 2020[27]) to the extent possible, as well as the DAC regional groupings (OECD, 2020[28]). Climate finance that is not allocable by region is grouped under "unspecified".

Table A C.5. List of developing countries and territories by region and sub-region

Region	Sub-region	Country
Africa	North Africa	Algeria, Egypt, Libya, Morocco, Tunisia
	East Africa	Burundi, Comoros, Djibouti, Eritrea, Ethiopia, Kenya, Madagascar, Malawi, Mauritius, Mozambique, Rwanda, Seychelles, Somalia, South Sudan, Sudan, Tanzania, Uganda, Zambia, Zimbabwe
	West Africa	Benin, Burkina Faso, Cabo Verde, Côte d'Ivoire, Gambia, Ghana, Guinea, Guinea-Bissau, Liberia, Mali, Mauritania, Niger, Nigeria, Saint Helena, Senegal, Sierra Leone, Togo
	Central Africa	Angola, Cameroon, Central African Republic, Chad, Congo, Democratic Republic of the Congo, Equatorial Guinea, Gabon, Sao Tome and Principe
	Southern Africa	Botswana, Eswatini, Lesotho, Namibia, South Africa
Asia	Central Asia	Armenia, Azerbaijan, Georgia, Kazakhstan, Kyrgyzstan, Tajikistan, Turkmenistan, Uzbekistan
	East Asia	Brunei Darussalam, Cambodia, China, Democratic People's Republic of Korea, Korea, Lao People's Democratic Republic, Indonesia, Malaysia, Mongolia, Philippines, Singapore, Thailand, Timor-Leste, Viet Nam
	South Asia	Afghanistan, Bangladesh, Bhutan, India, Maldives, Myanmar, Nepal, Pakistan, Sri Lanka
	Middle East	Bahrain, Iran, Iraq, Israel, Jordan, Kuwait, Lebanon, Oman, Qatar, Saudi Arabia, Syrian Arab Republic, Turkey, United Arab Emirates, West Bank and Gaza Strip, Yemen
Europe	N/A	Albania, Andorra, Belarus, Bosnia and Herzegovina, Kosovo, Moldova, Montenegro, North Macedonia, San Marino, Serbia, Ukraine
Americas	Central America	Belize, Costa Rica, El Salvador, Guatemala, Honduras, Mexico, Nicaragua, Panama
	South America	Argentina, Bolivia, Brazil, Chile, Colombia, Ecuador, Guyana, Paraguay, Peru, Suriname, Uruguay, Venezuela
	Caribbean	Antigua and Barbuda, Bahamas, Barbados, Cuba, Dominica, Dominican Republic, Grenada, Haiti, Jamaica, Montserrat, Saint Kitts and Nevis, Saint Lucia, Saint Vincent and the Grenadines, Trinidad and Tobago
Oceania	N/A	Cook Islands, Fiji, Kiribati, Marshall Islands, Micronesia, Nauru, Niue, Palau, Papua New Guinea, Samoa, Solomon Islands, Tokelau, Tonga, Tuvalu, Vanuatu, Wallis and Futuna

Source: (UNSD, 2020[27]), (OECD, 2020[28]).

The main divergences from the UN M49 standard in this report are that:

- Central Asia includes all post-soviet countries in Asia, except Russia, namely Armenia, Azerbaijan, Georgia, Kazakhstan, Kyrgyzstan, Tajikistan, Turkmenistan and Uzbekistan.
- Western Asia is replaced with the Middle East, whereas relevant post-soviet countries (Armenia, Azerbaijan, and Georgia) are included in Central Asia (see above).
- Sudan is included in Eastern Africa, rather than Northern Africa.

The main reason for these divergences is to ensure consistency with the DAC classification, which is used in the context of the underlying data on multilateral public and private finance mobilised. Moreover, provider countries (Table A C.1) and other countries and territories are excluded from the individual regions.

Although the regions identified often group countries and territories sharing specific attributes,[3] they differ significantly in terms of size, population, income, GNI, and other statistical categories. As a result, such regions should only be viewed as a tool that facilitates geographic analyses.

Income groups

The income group classification used in the context of the climate finance figures in this report is primarily based on the World Bank (WB) Country and Lending Groups classification (World Bank, 2020[13]) for 2018. With regards to territories that were included in the climate finance dataset but are not covered by the WB classification, namely the Cook Islands, Niue, Montserrat and Tokelau, the income group was retrieved from the DAC List of ODA Recipients for reporting on aid in 2018 and 2019 (OECD, 2020[14]).

Table A C.6. List of developing countries and territories by income group

Category	Countries
Low-income countries and territories (LICs)	Afghanistan, Benin, Burkina Faso, Burundi, Central African Republic, Chad, Democratic People's Republic of Korea, Democratic Republic of the Congo, Eritrea, Ethiopia, Gambia, Guinea, Guinea-Bissau, Haiti, Liberia, Madagascar, Malawi, Mali, Mozambique, Nepal, Niger, Rwanda, Sierra Leone, Somalia, South Sudan, Syrian Arab Republic, Tajikistan, Tanzania, Togo, Uganda, Yemen
Lower-middle income countries and territories (LMICs)	Angola, Bangladesh, Bhutan, Bolivia, Cabo Verde, Cambodia, Cameroon, Comoros, Congo, Côte d'Ivoire, Djibouti, Egypt, El Salvador, Eswatini, Ghana, Honduras, India, Indonesia, Kenya, Kiribati, Kyrgyzstan, Lao People's Democratic Republic, Lesotho, Mauritania, Micronesia, Moldova, Mongolia, Morocco, Myanmar, Nicaragua, Nigeria, Pakistan, Papua New Guinea, Philippines, Sao Tome and Principe, Senegal, Solomon Islands, Sudan, Timor-Leste, Tokelau, Tunisia, Ukraine, Uzbekistan, Vanuatu, Viet Nam, West Bank and Gaza Strip, Zambia, Zimbabwe
Upper-middle income countries and territories (UMICs)	Albania, Algeria, Argentina, Armenia, Azerbaijan, Belarus, Belize, Bosnia and Herzegovina, Botswana, Brazil, China, Colombia, Costa Rica, Cuba, Dominica, Dominican Republic, Ecuador, Equatorial Guinea, Fiji, Gabon, Georgia, Grenada, Guatemala, Guyana, Iran, Iraq, Jamaica, Jordan, Kazakhstan, Kosovo, Lebanon, Libya, Malaysia, Maldives, Marshall Islands, Mauritius, Mexico, Montenegro, Namibia, Nauru, North Macedonia, Paraguay, Peru, Saint Lucia, Saint Vincent and the Grenadines, Samoa, Serbia, South Africa, Sri Lanka, Suriname, Thailand, Tonga, Turkey, Turkmenistan, Tuvalu, Venezuela; Cook Islands, Montserrat, Niue, Saint Helena, Wallis and Futuna
High-income countries and territories (HICs)	Andorra, Antigua and Barbuda, Bahamas, Bahrain, Barbados, Brunei Darussalam, Chile, Israel, Korea, Kuwait, Oman, Palau, Panama, Qatar, Saint Kitts and Nevis, San Marino, Saudi Arabia, Seychelles, Singapore, Trinidad and Tobago, United Arab Emirates, Uruguay

Source: (World Bank, 2020[13]), (OECD, 2020[14]).

Notes

[1] Note by Turkey: The information in this document with reference to "Cyprus" relates to the southern part of the Island. There is no single authority representing both Turkish and Greek Cypriot people on the Island. Turkey recognises the Turkish Republic of Northern Cyprus (TRNC). Until a lasting and equitable solution is found within the context of the United Nations, Turkey shall preserve its position concerning the "Cyprus issue".

[2] Note by all the European Union Member States of the OECD and the European Union: The Republic of Cyprus is recognised by all members of the United Nations with the exception of Turkey. The information in this document relates to the area under the effective control of the Government of the Republic of Cyprus.

[3] For example, the Caribbean includes SIDS only. Similarly, Central Asia includes post-soviet states only, and Northern Africa Mediterranean countries.

Annex D. Sector groupings

The sectoral classification used in this report builds upon the classifications used in countries' biennial reports (BRs) to the UNFCCC as well as in the context of the OECD DAC and ECG statistics. Overall, builds upon the OECD DAC sectoral classification (OECD, 2020[29]). Table A D.1 presents the sector categories used in this report.

Table A D.1. Sectoral classification

Main sector group	Sector
Social infrastructure and services	Water and sanitation
	Other social infrastructure
Economic infrastructure and services	Banking and business services
	Energy
	Transport and storage
Production sectors	Agriculture, forestry and fishing
	Industry, mining and construction
Cross-cutting and multisector	General environmental protection
	Multisector
Other	Other

Note: "Other social infrastructure" includes education, health and population, support to government and civil society and other (e.g. social protection, housing, job creation, narcotics control, labour rights, etc.). "Other" includes activities that do not fit under the sectors listed.
Source: Adapted from (OECD, 2020[29]).

Data sources and links

Dedicated report webpage

http://oe.cd/cf-2013-18

Biennial Reports to the UNFCCC

https://unfccc.int/BRs

OECD Development Assistance Committee statistics and standards

http://oe.cd/RioMarkers

http://oe.cd/privfin

OECD Export Credit Group statistics and standards

www.oecd.org/trade/topics/export-credits

OECD Research Collaborative on Tracking Finance for Climate Action

www.oecd.org/env/researchcollaborative

OECD-IEA Climate Change Expert Group

http://oe.cd/ccxg

References

EUROSTAT (2019), *Enlargement countries - population statistics*, EUROSTAT, [12]
https://ec.europa.eu/eurostat/statistics-explained/index.php?title=Enlargement_countries_-
_population_statistics (accessed on 7 September 2020).

Falduto, C. and J. Ellis (2019), "Reporting Tables - potential areas of work under SBSTA and [22]
options - Part II: Financial support provided, mobilised and received", *OECD/IEA Climate
Change Expert Group Papers*, No. 2019/02, OECD Publishing, Paris,
https://dx.doi.org/10.1787/b0ba5a7e-en.

IPCC (2018), *Global warming of 1.5°C: Summary for Policymakers*, IPCC. [8]

MDBs (2020), *Joint Report on Multilateral Development Banks' 2019 Climate Finance*, [4]
https://www.ebrd.com/news/2020/mdbs-climate-finance-in-low-and-middleincome-countries-
in-2019-reaches-us-415-billion.html (accessed on 7 September 2020).

OECD (2020), *Amounts mobilised from the private sector for development*, [6]
http://www.oecd.org/dac/financing-sustainable-development/development-finance-
standards/mobilisation.htm (accessed on 9 September 2020).

OECD (2020), *Arrangement on Officially Supported Export Credits*, [25]
https://www.oecd.org/trade/topics/export-credits/arrangement-and-sector-understandings/
(accessed on 7 September 2020).

OECD (2020), *DAC and CRS code lists*, http://www.oecd.org/development/financing- [28]
sustainable-development/development-finance-standards/dacandcrscodelists.htm (accessed
on 7 September 2020).

OECD (2020), *DAC List of ODA Recipients*, http://www.oecd.org/dac/financing-sustainable- [14]
development/development-finance-standards/daclist.htm (accessed on 7 September 2020).

OECD (2020), *DAC Purpose Codes: sector classification*, [29]
http://www.oecd.org/development/financing-sustainable-development/development-finance-
standards/purposecodessectorclassification.htm (accessed on 22 September 2020).

OECD (2020), *The role of philanthropy in financing for development*, [17]
https://www.oecd.org/dac/financing-sustainable-development/development-finance-
standards/beyond-oda-foundations.htm (accessed on 2 July 2020).

OECD (2019), *Attribution of multilateral climate finance in the report "Climate Finance in 2013-14* [19]
and the USD 100 billion goal, https://www.oecd.org/environment/climate-finance-provided-
and-mobilised-by-developed-countries-in-2013-17-39faf4a7-en.htm.

OECD (2019), *Climate Finance Provided and Mobilised by Developed Countries in 2013-17*, [1]
OECD Publishing, Paris, https://dx.doi.org/10.1787/39faf4a7-en.

OECD (2019), *DAC: Amounts Mobilised from the Private Sector for Development*, https://www.oecd.org/dac/financing-sustainable-development/development-finance-standards/mobilisation.htm (accessed on 12 November 2019). [30]

OECD (2018), "Nominal exchange rates (vis-à-vis the US dollar)", in *OECD Economic Outlook, Volume 2018 Issue 1*, OECD Publishing, Paris, https://dx.doi.org/10.1787/eco_outlook-v2018-1-en. [26]

OECD (2016), *2020 Projections of Climate Finance Towards the USD 100 Billion Goal: Technical Note*, OECD Publishing, Paris, https://dx.doi.org/10.1787/9789264274204-en. [5]

OECD (2016), *OECD DAC Rio Markers for Climate Change: Handbook*, OECD Publishing, Paris, https://www.oecd.org/dac/environment-development/R. [18]

OECD (2015), *Climate Finance in 2013-14 and the USD 100 billion Goal: A Report by the OECD in Collaboration with Climate Policy Initiative*, OECD Publishing, Paris, https://dx.doi.org/10.1787/9789264249424-en. [2]

OECD DAC (2020), *Amounts Mobilised from the Private Sector for Development*, https://www.oecd.org/dac/financing-sustainable-development/development-finance-standards/mobilisation.htm. [7]

OECD DAC (2016), *Rio Markers for Climate: Handbook*, http://oe.cd/RioMarkers. [10]

OECD TOSSD (2020), *Total Official Support for Sustainable Development*, http://www.oecd.org/dac/tossd/ (accessed on 7 September 2020). [23]

TWG (2015), *Input to the OECD-CPI Report*, http://www.news.admin.ch/NSBSubscriber/message/attachments/41225.pdf. [24]

UN DESA (2019), *World Population Prospects 2019: Total Population - Both Sexes*, United Nations Department of Economic and Social Affairs. [11]

UNFCCC (2019), *Modalities, procedures and guidelines for the transparency framework for action and support referred to in Article 13 of the Paris Agreement*, https://unfccc.int/process-and-meetings/the-paris-agreement/paris-agreement-work-programme/katowice-climate-package. [3]

UNFCCC (2015), *Decision 9/CP.21: Methodologies for the reporting of financial information by Parties included in Annex I to the Convention, Report of the Conference of the Parties on its twenty-first session, held in Paris from 30 November to 11 December 2015.*, UNFCCC Secretariat, Bonn, https://unfccc.int/sites/default/files/resource/docs/2015/cop21/eng/10a02.pdf. [21]

UNFCCC (2015), *Paris Agreement*, UNFCCC, https://unfccc.int/process-and-meetings/the-paris-agreement/the-paris-agreement. [9]

UNFCCC (2012), *Decision 2/CP.17 Outcome of the work of the Ad Hoc Working Group on Long-term Cooperative Action under the Convention, Report of the Conference of the Parties on its seventeenth session, held in Durban from 28 November to 11 December 2011: Part Two: Action taken by the Conference of the Parties at its seventeenth session*, UNFCCC Secretariat, Bonn, https://unfccc.int/resource/docs/2011/cop17/eng/09a01.pdf#page=4. [20]

UN-OHRLLS (2020), *Least Developed Countries (LDCs)*, http://unohrlls.org/about-ldcs/ (accessed on 7 September 2020).

[16]

UN-OHRLLS (2020), *Small Island Developing States (SIDS)*, http://unohrlls.org/about-sids/ (accessed on 7 September 2020).

[15]

UNSD (2020), "M49 Standard", https://unstats.un.org/unsd/methodology/m49 (accessed on 7 September 2020).

[27]

World Bank (2020), *World Bank Country and Lending Groups*, https://datahelpdesk.worldbank.org/knowledgebase/articles/906519-world-bank-country-and-lending-groups (accessed on 7 September 2020).

[13]

www.ingramcontent.com/pod-product-compliance
Lightning Source LLC
Chambersburg PA
CBHW062029210326
41519CB00060B/7365